The Antiques Buyer

The
Antiques

Buyer

David Dickinson

Good Hunting

David Dickinson

ORION

For Christopher Haworth (1941–1995),
a great friend and colleague

I would like to convey my heartfelt thanks to Rosemary Kingsland.
Having just learned joined-up writing,
I would never have been able to create this book without her.

First published in 1999 by Orion

An imprint of Orion Books Ltd

Orion House, 5 Upper St Martin's Lane, London WC2H 9EA

Copyright © David Dickinson 1999

A CIP catalogue record for this book is available from the British Library.

ISBN 0-75281-831-7

Printed and bound in Italy

PICTURES SUPPLIED BY

Mary Evans Picture Library, Rex Features London, Christie's Images,
Bridgeman Art Library, Bonhams London, Sotheby's Picture Library.

Contents

Preface

Like many people, I first got interested in antiques as a young man when I bought a house, a place I could be proud of, that I wanted to furnish nicely. The family home that my wife, Lorne, and I bought happened to be a solid, small Edwardian house with a lot of character. It was in a mock-Tudor style with well-proportioned rooms, full skirting boards, dado rails, nice plaster cornices in the high ceilings and good fireplaces.

It was the kind of house that, while not as grand as a stately mansion, still had great possibilities. It was a house crying out for nice period pieces, in this case, late Victorian or Edwardian, that wouldn't cost an arm and a leg to buy. So in this sense, the house itself inspired my passion for antiques.

But I was young, certainly not wealthy, and definitely very green when it came to knowing how and where to acquire the kind of furniture and decorative items within my budget that I instinctively knew would do this handsome little house of ours justice. I knew what I wanted, I knew what I could afford, but where on earth did I start?

My first ventures and journey of discovery as I dipped my toes into the world of antiques with its mystery and closely guarded secrets, ultimately led to a new career and a life-long commitment to and passion for the subject. I wasn't born with that knowledge, nobody is. Through trial and error, I learned, and so, too, can you. For you, I hope this book might take out some of the trial and a lot of the error!

David Dickinson

Introduction

My early experience of going to antiques shops, going to sales, going to fairs, looking, touching, getting my hands on, not being scared to ask questions, perhaps making one or two mistakes along the way, but all the time soaking it up like a sponge and learning, learning, learning, served to 'get my eye in'. It was also great fun.

Getting your eye in sums up how you can become an expert, how you can gain knowledge and appreciation until you reach that sublime point when you look at a piece and instinctively know that 'it stands right'. This book will be full of terms like that, which are used in the antiques trade and which best describe what I want to say, and I will explain their meaning in detail as we progress.

You can't often have an expert with you when you go shopping for antiques, but that's what I want to try to be. I want to take some of the stress out of your learning process by metaphorically taking your hand and guiding you through the exciting world of antiques, step by step, showing you how to formulate your taste, how to get your eye in, and how to go about buying the pieces you want. I'll also elaborate on the basic points of restoration; whether to restore or not, at what stage restoration becomes too much, and the essential differences between the real thing, a reproduction and a fake.

You might already have started to collect antiques. Perhaps you have gone to a car boot sale, or poked about in a junk shop, or gone into little shops in some historic old town while on holiday, places such as Bath or Harrogate or Hay-on-Wye, and bought something small and charming. But the idea of going to an auction and buying something larger and more expensive might scare you to death, in which case you might have questions such as: 'How do I bid?'; 'Suppose I scratch my nose and stitch myself up with a wildly expensive painting I can't afford?'; 'What does the buyer's premium mean?'; 'How can I tell if that object is any good?' or 'How much is it really worth?'.

This book won't go into great detail on the antiques themselves by telling you how many different kinds of dove-tailed joints there are, or the difference between Louis XV and George III commodes, because there are plenty of books already, written by experts in this or that field, which you can buy or get from the library, on every subject from porcelain to carpets, clocks to barometers. (I've included an extensive reading list on page 187.) But what this book *will* teach you are a few professional skills. It will, I hope, also answer your questions about how to make the best buys, where to go to buy antiques and how to avoid pitfalls, in a sensible and straightforward way.

In this book I will act as your mentor at each stage, advising you what to do and what questions to ask, so that each time you are about to dig deep in your pocket and buy some antique object, you can make a sensible, informed decision. By following this advice when you are buying, and remember, you will be doing all the work, you will soak up knowledge and gain an appreciation of what is 'good' and what is 'bad'. In time, through your own efforts and perseverance, you will discover that your taste has been formulated almost subconsciously. And your taste is important: you really do have to develop your own style and know what you like. It's no good buying a mishmash of objects which someone else thinks are wonderful if you loathe them. After all, you are buying for your home, as I first started out buying for mine, and you're the one who has to live with the object.

I don't promise to make you an expert, nor can I distil 25 years' experience of buying and selling antiques into 180 pages. But what I can do, using that experience, is explain the ups and downs; the do's and don'ts, the hows and the whys and many other aspects of the business. I can tell you some good sound, sensible ground rules and tips that other books don't give you and that will make the learning process exciting and enjoyable. If I knew 25 years ago what I know now, if I'd had at my fingertips all the knowledge in this book that I'm passing on to you, I could have saved myself lots of disappointment and money along the way and that's what I hope I'll do for you.

By offering examples from my own experience, generalizing and giving simple explanations, I hope people will quickly grasp the fundamentals of antiques hunting. It's a bit like cookery. Some cooks offer such complicated recipes and techniques to novice cooks that they're likely to be put off for life. But you've only got to watch Delia Smith's simple direct approach and compare her method with the more flowery patter of the cordon bleu people with all their little bowls containing this or that to see that. Fascinating though the latter are to watch, there's something so essentially sensible and basic about the way she explains things, that she makes you think, 'Yes, I think I could tackle that.'

So overall, this book might be described as the Delia Smith approach, a 'back-to-basics' look at the subject of buying antiques: first learn to boil an egg and in due course you'll be making perfect soufflés.

Good luck, and happy hunting!

chapter 1

The Joy of Antiques

I want to begin by teaching the basics of buying antiques, whether for your own home or for collection or for resale, very much following the path that I took.

It's interesting how you develop, how you have an affinity for certain things without even thinking about it or knowing where it comes from. I have always loved nice things in life. I get my love of style and luxury from my French grandmother and my passion for the flamboyant and for trading from my Armenian grandfather. I think I baffled my grandmother with my early instinctive astuteness in the trading game.

At school I was always swapping marbles and generally trading small things as a matter of course. And although we didn't have a car, I was always looking at other people's and admiring them. I can remember running alongside particularly flash cars, not with any degree of envy, but saying, 'Mister, it's magnificent! Can I have a look at it?' I wanted to taste all the experiences and learn about the very best, never from an envious point of view but because I admired it.

My French grandmother, who was a good old-fashioned stick, believed that you either had a trade or you were a white-collar worker. She'd been through the war years and had seen men dealing in the black market. To her, traders like these were just spivs, and seeing where my interest lay, and, I think, to save me from that, she put me into a factory. She was a decent, hard-working woman, who wanted me to have a trade in my hands. She had no idea what the term 'entrepreneur' meant, didn't pause to consider that other kinds of traders, such as stockbrokers, were highly successful and respectable people.

I started buying for myself in a small way with jam pans and small oak chairs, selling them on to other dealers, perhaps making a few pounds; but I always had big eyes. Even if I couldn't afford the best quality *then*, I always thought that some day I would be up there with the big boys. My natural inclination, when I was bidding for the coal scuttle was to look longingly at the Georgian table. I'd say to myself, 'I think it's wonderful and I want to buy it, and some day I will.'

But, although I had a taste for beautiful things in those early days, I didn't have any knowledge of the styles of master designers. I didn't know a Chippendale from a Hepplewhite; while if someone had mentioned the work of fine English cabinet maker, Gillows of Lancaster, I'd have looked at them blankly. And I would have been astonished at the idea that one day I would actually *buy* such pieces, and for very large sums of money.

My interest in furniture really got going when we bought a house. I was brought up in the working- to middle-class area of Cheadle Heath, Manchester. As a boy I used to go to the park at Bramhall and always thought it quite a posh area, so when Lorne and I married and rented a house in Bramhall, I thought I was going up in the world. Then one day I was driving down a lane and I saw a 'for sale' sign outside an attractive little Edwardian house. I turned around and went back to get Lorne and we knocked on the door.

When the owner, a retired schoolteacher, answered you could tell she was wondering who we were in our hippyish outfits, me with my hair down to my shoulders and Lorne still in her carpet slippers. I asked if we could have a look round. 'You should really book an appointment with the estate agent,' she said doubtfully. I said, 'Madam, we are very serious people.' She smiled and let us in. Within half an hour, I turned to her and said, 'We'll have it.'

The asking price was £8,650. This elderly lady said, 'Are you sure you can afford it?' Full of the confidence of youth, I assured her, 'No problem.' She looked astounded. I think that was the only time in my life that I didn't haggle. We had a 10 per cent deposit and managed to arrange a mortgage. Very quickly, the house was ours.

Now came my first big mistake. Looking back, I think it was probably lack of knowledge and money that caused it. The schoolteacher was selling the entire contents of her house, and some of her things were lovely old pieces such as a bureau, bookcases and tables. She gave us first refusal and we chose one or two items. The rest went to the local antiques dealer, lock, stock and barrel. Once we moved in, of course we needed basic pieces of furniture: tables and chairs and perhaps a sideboard of some sort. At first we scoured modern shops, where we saw nothing we liked, and we quickly moved to looking in our local antiques shops.

In all honesty, I wouldn't have recognized a Victorian piece as being one, and I certainly wouldn't have been able to tell the difference between Victorian and Edwardian, but recalling how 'right' the schoolteacher's period furniture had looked, as soon as I saw similar pieces I knew that that style was exactly right for our new house.

Why antiques?

I know lots of people who have lovely new houses, and they go out and buy a brand-new, beautifully made dining-room suite that appeals to them. It's expensive and they are the first owners – buying it is just like purchasing a shiny new car.

I could understand this if what they buy is bang up-to-date in look by a modern designer – Phillippe Starke for example. But if what they buy is not contemporary, but reproduction furniture, my feeling is that it's probably because they like the period look and the style of the period that has been reproduced. In this case, I am convinced that if these people thought about the issue, or, more to the point, even knew enough about it, for their money they would prefer to have the genuine article, if they could afford it, or at least, an original antique. It simply might not occur to some people that they can buy nice, well-made period furniture. Antiques shops are for other people, they might think; or antiques are too expensive. Or they might be frightened by the process involved, perhaps of displaying a lack of knowledge. I can recall how when I was young antiques shops were terrifying places where only the very posh and the very rich dared step over the portals and I never dreamed I could negotiate a price. But it's worth overcoming these preconceptions and fears, by taking the time to learn more because when you buy an antique, you are buying so much more than just something old.

If you go into any modern furniture shop today and buy a so-called 'traditional' dining-room suite it will be in one of several styles. Most of the designs available are originally from another period. But the wood used is likely to be not so good, because timber of the same quality as that used in the original period is too expensive or not available in the mass market, and often what is used is laminated contiboard. Nor is the workmanship likely to be a patch on the original. The mass-market factory does not use the same

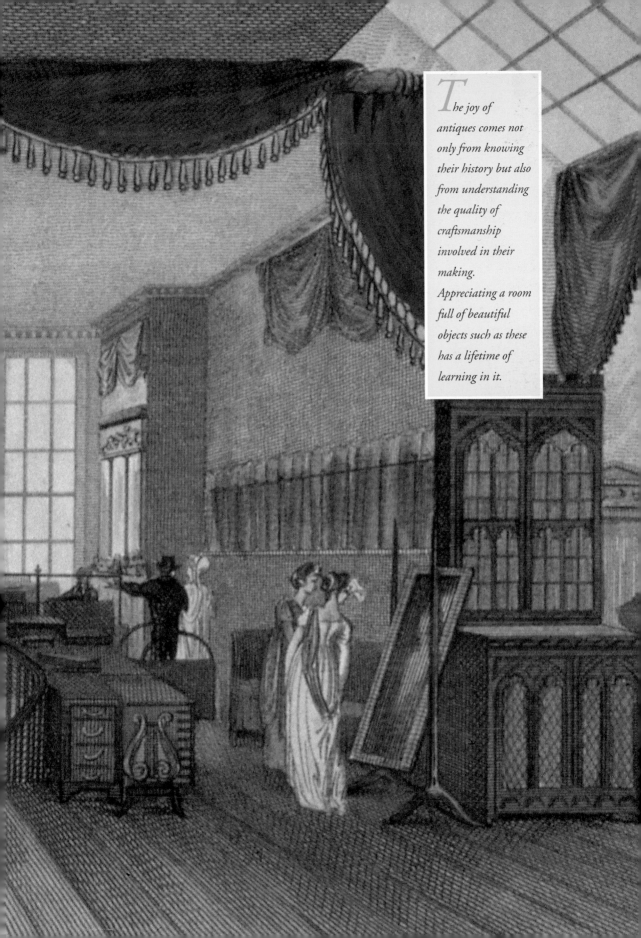

The joy of antiques comes not only from knowing their history but also from understanding the quality of craftsmanship involved in their making. Appreciating a room full of beautiful objects such as these has a lifetime of learning in it.

*S*tages in the upholstery of an armchair from Diderot's
Encyclopedie *of 1760. Use of the best materials and the
craftsman's skill and patience has created furniture that has
stood the test of time.*

techniques as the old craftsmen, who dedicated their lives to excellence, because to use them today is too expensive. I know that there are people making reproduction furniture today to very high standards, but often the pieces they produce are very expensive and their pieces often cost far more than antiques because the cost of labour is so high. As soon as you take a piece of reproduction furniture from the shop its value is reduced by at least two-thirds; whereas with an antique the chances are that when you come to sell you will get most of your money back and sometimes even make a profit.

In the 18th century, when you had money you would go to the best people, whether for clothing or for furniture. You would go to them because of their reputation. Thomas Chippendale could be found in a certain street which was fashionable amongst furniture makers, so you would go to inspect his workshop. You would see a team of carvers and polishers going about their work and you would probably stand and think, 'By Jove, these people know how to make furniture!' And I suppose if you go to the workshops of modern-day couturiers, you would feel the same. They choose from the finest fabrics and accessories, beads, sequins, bones for the bodices. They wouldn't dream of using the cheapest stuff that's on the market; you can't charge several thousand pounds for a cocktail dress and make it out of inferior material, because it shows and if you did you soon wouldn't have many customers left.

If you think along those lines with furniture, comparing the methods of the 18th century to those of the modern day, you'll understand what I mean. As with couture outfits, there are of course still people producing 'couture' furniture. You could go to Lord Linley, for example, and find that with the furniture he makes, he employs techniques that were used in the 18th century, perhaps mechanized for speed, and he uses the very best source material available. However, there are very few Linleys around, his furniture is expensive and at the end of the day his particular style is a matter of taste and might not be your cup of tea.

Although I'm talking about furniture, the principle is the same for all antiques. When you buy a genuine, good-quality antique it is really exciting because not only are you buying a style that you like (as with reproduction furniture) you are buying something that was at the time the very best available (which you are unlikely to be able to do with reproduction furniture) – and you are also buying a slice of history.

With furniture, if the craftsman has started off with the right ingredients – the right types of timber, the right types of veneer that decorate these tim-

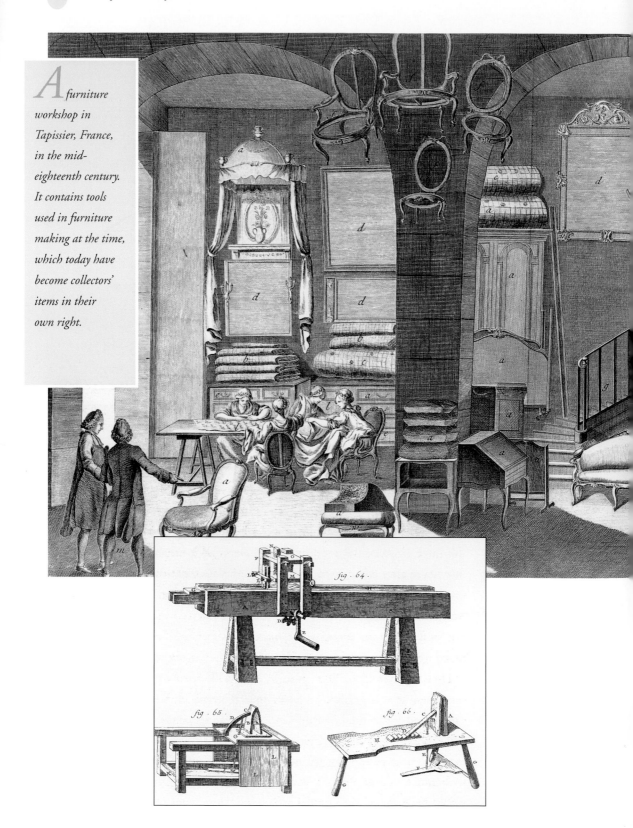

A furniture workshop in Tapissier, France, in the mid-eighteenth century. It contains tools used in furniture making at the time, which today have become collectors' items in their own right.

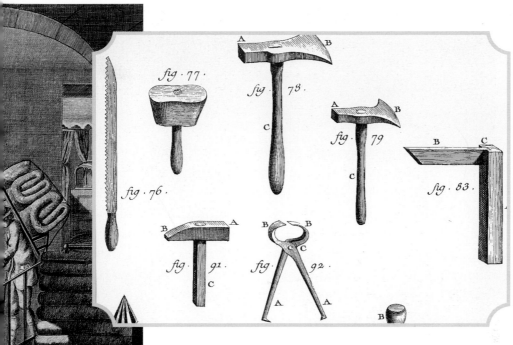

bers, the right gilt or ormolu decoration, solid brass handles and so forth – the quality of the finished piece shines out. Because of this original care, many pieces of antique furniture haven't deteriorated in over 100 years, through all manner of climatic conditions. They haven't dramatically expanded or contracted, cracked or broken – whereas had they been made with lesser materials and workmanship they would have done so.

You can find out more about construction in deeper detail in specialist books – it would certainly take this entire book to get below the surface of this huge subject – but essentially, because wood is organic and continues to move even after being sawn, the stability of a piece of furniture is all down to the care that was taken in the making. In a fine antique, the raw ingredients would have been properly seasoned timbers, and as a result the carcass does not shift within six months, expand or contract half an inch; nor will the joints work against each other, dragging themselves out of alignment.

However, not all antique furniture is good. Even in the 18th and 19th centuries, as today, there were manufacturers of different standards, and some used lower qualities of timber and veneers and accessories and so forth, because of the cost. Not all cabinet-makers would have been working for rich entrepreneurs or aristocrats; some worked for more modest people with not much money. As with high-street clothing manufacturers, they would have copied the grander styles, in cheaper timber or thinner veneers.

In the salerooms, a century or more later, you can spot these cheaper pieces, perhaps because the veneer has bubbled and peeled away, or the piece just doesn't 'sit right'.

What do you want?

You don't necessarily have to know very much about antiques, or any particular subject, come to that, in order to know what you, personally, like.

To someone who is about to start looking for antique furniture I don't think I would say: 'Ah, we'll go for a grand town piece', or 'We'll go for a decorative piece', or 'We'll go for a country piece.' Instead, I would ask them what they wanted. You should ask yourself this. If you don't know, I would suggest that you first look at a whole range of books or catalogues to find out what excites you, then go out and about and look at the real things. That will give you the first glimmerings of price and quality and style, and from there you can start to formulate your own taste.

The kind of knowledge I acquired in those first days, as a lot of people do, was gained by visiting my local antiques shops and salerooms and looking for something that was visually appealing to me. If a piece had a particularly rich patina and colour, (I didn't even know that the word 'patina' meant the pleasing surface gloss, built up over years and centuries of use and wear and polishes, that dealers refer to as 'the skin') I would stroke the wood and say to Lorne: 'Well, that's a nice old table. I don't know what it is, but it looks a good old solid job. What a nice colour. It's solid wood, it's attractive, and I like the style.' Looking at a set of chairs, I didn't know if they were Chippendale-style or what, but it was quite clear to me that they were lovely and nicely carved.

Without realising it, I was homing in on a fundamental point. In noting what an item was made of, whether it was mahogany or oak, and whether it was good-looking, I was finding out what touched me in a personal way.

I would go home with the piece of furniture in mind, I would weigh up the space it would fit and try to visualize it standing there. In this, decoration played its part. How would it look with that height of ceiling, that carpet or those curtains?

I'd always fancied a grandfather clock and after we'd bought essentials such as tables and chairs, we looked for a clock. I learned that they were called 'long-case clocks' (though to me, 'grandfather clock' has a nice comfortable sound to it), and from there I widened my scope and moved on to seek out other things that I personally wanted and would enjoy owning.

So to find out what you like, I suggest you have a good old nose around, going to antiques fairs, antique shops, the occasional auction, perhaps an exhibition or in market-places. There you can check out a broad range of goods in an enjoyable and often exciting way. This shouldn't be a grand academic exercise and you don't need an art degree for it. What you are doing essentially is looking for pieces that appeal, to decorate your home with.

Don't necessarily rush, but you don't have to take years about this either. Suppose you're looking for a dining-room table or chairs: what style are you going to choose? Where do you live, what size of room have you got, what's going to suit you? What type of timber appeals to you? Do you like oak, mahogany or rosewood, or perhaps walnut and satinwood? All these woods have a different look or feel to them, and often they come from different periods, for example, with English furniture, Elizabethan or Jacobean is nearly always oak, Queen Anne is often walnut and Georgian is usually mahogany. Whatever you are looking for, and I can't stress this enough, *you have got to buy something that you particularly like*, and looking at pieces is how you'll find out what this is.

I specialize in and have a special affection for 19th century furniture of exhibition quality. You might prefer more rustic country oak pieces, or furniture in Sheraton style. You might like Victorian Gothic, or painted French pieces. Or perhaps furniture is not your first love, you might want to collect clocks or porcelain or bronzes. Whatever your interest, *remember, it's your taste, it's what you want that matters.* If you go out and buy a little writing desk and bring it back to your home, then sit and work at it with a keen sense of pleasure, you have achieved something very special. It's your find, your little treasure.

If there are any rules in the antiques business for the first-time buyer, the first rule would be *buy what gives you enjoyment and what pleases your eye.* That's why you're buying; after all, you're going to live with what you buy.

I would never tell you to buy anything with investment in mind unless you have every intention of selling the items quite soon; otherwise you might well end up with things you have to live with for a long time while they appreciate in value, objects that you might come to loathe and have no earthly use for. The investment side should be secondary to owning something beautiful that gives you a great deal of pleasure and if it appreciates in value – well, that's an added bonus.

So you want to collect....

Lf I were asked to advise somebody who wanted to start collecting antiques but hadn't won the lottery I'd have to consider their tastes, their interests and their reasons to collect. These are different for everyone. Somebody might have been left a collection of silver Apostle spoons in a will and start from that point. They wouldn't necessarily start collecting spoons; the gift might have inspired an interest in collecting silver that turns into a life-long interest. Someone else might spot a tortoiseshell box at an antiques fair and think, 'Yes, I like this. I think I'll start collecting small boxes', perhaps becoming like one lady I know in Scotland who started with one broken box that she carefully restored and now has several hundreds of every shape and size. In Bramhall, I once went to a home of a man who was a collector of mechanical musical boxes. His collection had grown from an interest to a total obsession. I had never seen anything like it. In the centre of the living room in his modern bungalow was a three-piece suite and a television, and the rest of the room was lined shoulder-to-shoulder with free-standing penny-in-the-slot polyphones. He'd even built an extension which was lined with floor-to-ceiling wooden shelving crammed with huge musical boxes. The whole house was taken over and his family had to somehow live in the middle of it.

Some people are addicted to tea pots, others are besotted by old cars. In fact, you can collect anything, including shoes and ships and sealing wax. My advice to collectors, whatever they are collecting, would be, as always, choose what you like.

Of all the areas of collecting, my particular area of expertise, furniture, is one that appeals to most people. We all have to have furniture in our homes. Some of us might have been lucky enough to have inherited a lot or a few nice pieces and it is that which sets them off on the antique furniture trail. Others might have bought new or second-hand furniture (and by second-hand, I mean recycled modern items, such as tables and chairs and lamp stands) and want to replace them with antiques. Or, perhaps, like me, you started off with good, but modestly priced Edwardian and Victorian pieces and, as you learn more, or as your income expands, you want to replace them with some magnificent Regency or Georgian pieces.

2

Starting Out

Looking for quality

Ⅰf there was one thing only I could leave you with after reading this book it would be simply this: buy quality. Looking back over my 25 years or so, what has stood me in good stead throughout my career, without question, is buying quality. Sometimes, on the day, this seemed a little expensive, but it's been my experience that quality will never let you down. Before you go out into the market-place to actually buy something, you need to learn how to assess quality, which is what this chapter is about.

I can walk into a room and see at a glance everything I need to know about the contents of that room. I know from experience from years of looking at tables, chairs and corner cupboards when something is 'good'. I'm looking for something to catch my attention, something that's got flair about it and when it's there, I spot it at once. Sometimes a piece of furniture will draw me like a magnet; it will seem to scream 'quality' at me, even if it looks tired, or, as in a recent case of a table at a small country auction, it has a piece of chipped and paint-stained plywood glued to the top of four very scruffy, albeit mahogany, legs. In the catalogue the estimated price was given as £400–£600; but my eye recognized it as a once-fine Georgian library table that could, with a little care, be restored to its former glory.

And so it proved. A handful of dealers in that auction room were on to that neglected table like bees around a honey pot and despite its battered state it went for £15,000. With restoration and adding on a margin for profit, eventually it would have been sold through some smart antiques shop for anything up to £25,000, not bad for a piece of 'junk'.

Conversely, I was in a Mayfair auction house recently where a famous person had put the contents of his several homes up for sale, and a piece screamed at me, but this time not because it was an undiscovered treasure but because it was so awful! It was marked up in the catalogue with an estimate of several thousands of pounds, but possibly the only original thing about that red lacquer cabinet on a stand was the carcass of the bottom half. Most of the rest of it, the highly decorative gold Chinese-style painting and the mother-of-pearl inlay, was very recent and poorly executed. I imagine that the celebrity had been nudged into buying it by some fashionable and expensive interior decorator who might be very good at matching paint with fabric but hadn't necessarily a clue about antiques.

Sometimes my first quick glance doesn't hold up when I get closer to the article. Recently, I spotted what I took to be a fine military portrait from across a scruffy little saleroom. It had a very low estimate in the catalogue and I felt that familiar quickening of the pulse, thinking I might have come across a small undiscovered treasure. But when I got closer, I was disappointed. It was a late Victorian photograph that had been painted over with oils, called an oliograph. Now, you might not have spotted that. However, if you had, and had asked the auctioneer the right questions, I have no doubt at all that you would have been given an accurate description. Armed with the truth, you might even have decided to buy it: for £60 or £80 it would make a nice decorative picture for your wall.

At the other end of the scale, at a major sale I spotted a black lacquer cabinet and didn't have to get close to know that it was a real dog. It jumped out at me and practically bit me from six feet; but it was superficially attractive and flamboyant, the kind of decorative piece that style magazines are recommending at the moment to jazz up simplistic interiors, so anyone with less experience might have been taken in by its exotic lacquerwork and mother-of-pearl inlay. You have to remember all that glitters is not gold. Such a piece, if authentic, would sell for £60,000. The estimate in the catalogue was £25,000 which should ring a warning bell, far too cheap on the one hand for a real quality piece and far too expensive on the other hand for the mish-mash it was.

I wouldn't have it at any price, because I couldn't do anything with it. To me that piece would just be heartache and pain. If I took it to a fair the vetters would throw it off my stand. A dealer couldn't put it in his shop and sell it with a guarantee because he'd be inviting trouble. Somebody with money wouldn't want it, and even as a dog's dinner it would be more than somebody with little money could afford.

Becoming an expert in the field of antiques, being able to recognize quality when you see it from 6m (20ft) is not a gift you are born with, but something anyone can acquire with perseverance and practice, and you won't acquire it if you let interior decorators, or indeed anyone else, choose for you. It's something you've got to do yourself.

Get on the learning curve

Once you've got an idea of what you're interested in, you'll need to learn about it, and that's when you'll start discovering what wonderful subjects antiques are. Let me tell you about my own passion, furniture, and you'll see what I mean.

The furniture I look out for is, more specifically, exhibition-quality pieces from 1800 to 1910, which takes in the Regency, the reign of William IV, the long Victorian period from the 1830s right the way through until 1901 and the Edwardian period from 1901 to 1910. (All through this book you'll find me referring to the furniture of this period. You may be interested in other types of antiques but the principles of buying furniture are the same as those for buying any antiques, so bear with me, I might convert you to my passion by the end anyway!)

There are all kinds of furniture movements within that time-frame, overlapping each other and sometimes copying earlier styles. There are huge influences, from Greek, Persian and Egyptian to Chinese. The Victorians were hard-working and had a definite sense of their own identity, their importance in the world and where they were going, and of course their period covered a great time-span – from a relatively simple age (technologically) right through the Industrial Revolution and into the 20th century. The Industrial Revolution brought about tremendous new-found wealth and a new type of society – the *nouveau riche*. The former labour-intensive hands-on processes in furniture making gave way to more mechanized, but still very high-quality methods. Furniture making reached a stage where it still used the exceptional materials, and had the expert, quality craftsmen from the earlier age but also had all the advantages of the modern up-to-date techniques which helped to produce very fine pieces of furniture with great tolerance, and crisper lines and inlays than had been produced before. In order to display the new expertise of the age – not just with furniture making – from about the 1850s on there were a succession of grand International Exhibitions such as that held in 1851 at Crystal Palace near London, and others held in Vienna, Paris and Rome.

There is also furniture made within this time that takes its form and shape and design from the 18th century, but is not an exact copy. It's rather like a craftsman has looked at, say, a piece of Sheraton furniture and made something that takes inspiration from it but has a 19th century feel, with additions that are only to be found in the 19th century. Pieces inspired by the past like this are called *inspirational pieces* and were made in other periods too. A lot of designs of this kind are neo-classical; in the 18th century, designers made wonderful break-fronted bookcases with Palladium tops, taking their inspiration from the ancient world of Greece or Rome and the great architectural heritage to be found there.

In 1760, when a bookcase with a Palladium top was made, the people in the great houses didn't say to themselves, 'That comes from Greek or Roman design.' They just enjoyed it. A lot of the furniture made in the Regency period reverts to this great classical period, too, such as that made for the Brighton Pavilion. It is all such wonderful, decorative furniture that you can't helped being uplifted and inspired just by being around it.

In the early 19th century – the period named after the Prince Regent – there was still the strong brown English furniture made of mahogany as there was in the 18th century, but there was much more flamboyance of gilded decoration because the Prince Regent himself was a very flamboyant, unusual character, to say the least, and he inspired a style of highly decorative furniture that re-introduced Roman and Greek motifs. This overlapping of influences, like circles on a lake, has gone on right up until today. You can walk into a modern furniture shop and see a key pattern in a table, for example, that you can trace back to Greece.

Some styles are quite unique, such as the Arts and Crafts movement which has a distinct look; but many are revivals, such as the Gothic revival led by Pugin. Much of this is based on the romantic medieval age of chivalry; you could as well call it an Arthurian or even a medieval revival. All these revivals and influences keep on following each other.

If you are going to understand antiques, if you are going to know what makes a particular piece 1820 (Regency) and not 1850 (Victorian), you are going to have to get in on this learning curve. And that's just in the British Isles. There's all of Europe, America which was building its own furniture right from the time of the *Mayflower*, and you can get quite esoteric in your interests by studying Chinese antiques (which influenced furniture as well as

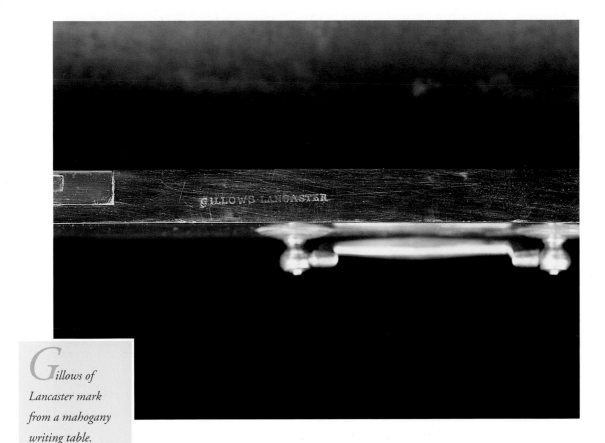

Gillows of Lancaster mark from a mahogany writing table.

pottery and porcelain, hence Thomas Chippendale's chinoiserie look, which means 'of the Chinese') or Japanese and Russian, also huge fields.

In their day, furniture-making firms like Gillows and Hollands had six or seven hundred men and boys working in their factory; and men with 30 years' experience in their hands would pass on their knowledge to the boys. I remember starting at a factory myself, as a boy of fifteen, going to do a year as an apprentice. I can still remember going to what was called the tool room, where the *crème de la crème* of engineers worked. They didn't wear blue overalls, they had white coats; and they made the jigs and tools. These men had wonderful skills which awed and fascinated me, and which they passed on to apprentices just as the men did in those 18th-century furniture workshops and factories. They'd have departments: one man would only work on carcasses, one man would veneer. In the veneer department, the wood was cut into very thin slices from a plank and laid out in batches. It's fascinating to think of those beautiful veneers from different trees around the world, pegged on lines like X-ray plates. The most skilled man of all paired and matched them. Each side of a bookcase or bureau got matching veneers.

A George III satinwood occasional table. Banded in rosewood and inlaid with ebony and boxwood stringing, it is particularly elegant in style.

OPPOSITE *a Regency mahogany bedside commode and a Regency 'plum pudding' mahogany commode. Both pieces were produced by Gillows of Lancaster.*

It was not a question of 'Fred! Take that one, that one and that one.' They'd hold them up and very carefully select: 'Right, those for the front panels, those for the drawers, those for the sides.' In another department there'd be a man who did the marquetry (inlaying ornamentation into a piece of another material, such as ivory). He would probably spend 20 years learning until he could probably do it blindfolded.

There are furniture makers still, individual craftsmen who are brilliant. Over the years I have known one or two wood carvers who are magically talented, when they get out their carving tools. It's just unbelievable what they can produce. Probably after 30 years of work they could become a Grinling Gibbons; but mostly they work in the restoration business. I am thinking, for example, of some of the quite stupendous work that went into replacing the Grinling Gibbons' carving in the state apartments at Hampton Court after the fire there; or the workmanship in the restoration of Windsor Castle after the devastating fire there. When you are replacing the work of the past, your individual talents are not necessarily to the forefront, even if you are a great artist and craftsman.

Studying all this and learning about it is not a simplistic thing: it's magnificent. And that's just the furniture of a particular period. There is such a richness and wealth to discover in all aspects from china to paintings that anyone who gets interested in the field of antiques is likely to become hooked for life.

Learning to look

Recognizing quality time after time comes from what I call 'getting your eye in'. People like myself – antique dealers, art experts whatever – we have all 'got our eye in'. When I see many objects in a sale I mentally start to grade them into As, Bs and Cs, as if I'm marking exam papers. It becomes second nature to do this, whatever your field. A gardener will always spot the best dahlia or rose in a flower show. Years ago, when blacksmiths regularly shoed horses, any blacksmith worth his salt could look at a horseshoe and tell you in seconds how good it was, and even whose work it was. Likewise, a skilled wood carver recognizes another carver's work, even if he has never met them. All these people have got their eye in.

Remember, you don't have to be an expert to judge poor workmanship. But in order to recognise expertise and learn to judge what makes one antique article better than another, you have to hone your eye.

At first, this seems an impossible task. You think you'll never get the hang of it. How does this table with straight legs compare with that table with round legs? Perhaps one table seats ten and costs £600, while another table seats six and costs £1000 – why? Was it because one was in shop in a more fashionable district than the other, or was it to do with age, the type of wood it was made from, the workmanship or the style? Here are a couple of tips:

● **Look** AT AS MUCH AS YOU CAN. The best place to start looking and learning is a big, antiques fair, because you usually have a couple of hundred top dealers gathered in one room or location. By a top dealer I mean someone who has a great deal of experience, because a newcomer or a novice dealer won't be able to afford the very high rents for the stands. And there is a way of stopping high pressure sales. If you're on a stand and someone rushes at you with 'Can we help you?', reply, 'Not at the moment, thank you. But may I have a look at your lovely things?'

A grand fair, such as the annual Olympia fair, would suit your needs better than a small, country one, simply because there are so many more quality examples on show (see page 69 for more on fairs).

Or say you are looking for a walnut spoon-backed chair. Look in trade magazines (see page 82) to see if there are any antiques fairs within easy reach. Check out your local antiques shops. If you have only one or two small ones locally, the chances are that you won't find one spoon-backed chair, let alone the several you'll need to make comparisons, so treat yourself to a day trip or a weekend away in a town where you know you'll find plenty of antiques shops. You could even stroll around a stately home, where you will certainly find marvellous furniture, the only drawback being that no price tags will be attached to the items on display, and neither will you be permitted to crawl over them.

● **Choose** YOUR SUBJECT. Decide what you want to learn about that day, remembering that you can't cram it all in one go. Suppose you go to a fair and decide to focus on marquetry furniture. If the fair is worth its salt, it won't take long before you have spotted at least three similar examples. By looking and comparing them and using common sense, you will quickly separate them into average, reasonable and superb examples.

How to look

Go over the pieces, point-by-point methodically. If it's a piece of furniture, for instance, look at the main decorative panels on the tops, and compare the wood, the colour, the quality and craftsmanship of the marquetry. Ask yourself questions. Is it fine or is it crude, do you spot tell-tale gaps along the side of the inlay where perhaps the craftsman hasn't trimmed the wood to a perfect fit? Does the design flow and gel? Do you say to yourself, 'This is stunning. How on earth did they do that?' Look at the side panels, look at the front. Again look at the quality of the inlay. Is the cutting out of the woods and fit of the other pieces laid in absolutely perfect? Are there any gaping holes or dark marks where the maker has had to fill in?

Suppose the piece of furniture that you are studying has no inlay. The same rules apply. Does it look right? Does it stand right? Is the wood satisfying to look at? Do the proportions of the piece make your heart sing, even though you don't yet know why? With a lot of furniture, even simple furniture, you can open the drawers or the doors, and look at the construction inside, at the shelves, and at the way everything fits. You can see whether it has been beautifully made. It doesn't have to be the most expensive piece, but by using good common sense you can say to yourself: 'This is well made. I like the colour of the veneer on the outside, it all fits very flush and everything about it is pleasing.'

Now moving on from marquetry, look at other pieces of furniture. Find pieces that have mouldings, or carved or turned legs. Compare one set of carvings with another. You may see that one in comparison to another doesn't have the sharpness, the clarity about it. The first has wonderfully crisp carving; it looks organic, it is a much nicer thing. Your eyes will tell you these things and so by constantly making comparisons you learn.

Remember, at a big fair every piece is vetted by a team of experts in all the different fields. Nothing escapes their attention because the fair's reputation is at stake. So you can be confident that what it says on the tag or what you are told by the dealer is guaranteed and is as accurate as possible. Bear in mind also that a reputable and experienced dealer does not buy rubbish, and so does not have rubbish to sell.

At the very least, you'll have a nice interesting day out. What you are actually doing is building up your knowledge, getting a feel for many different kinds of antiques, building up a picture of the market so that you will be able to make a general valuation for this or that piece from one period or another. You're beginning to get a good idea of what antiques are worth. You're looking at *quality* and *condition*. You're noticing that one chair has got its original little pot casters (that is, they are made of white pottery and have brass fittings) while another might have iron casters that you notice are not as attractive. Almost without knowing it, you're taking it all in and beginning to make judgements.

It is impossible to tell you what to be on the look out for in terms of good original pieces. I could tell you, for instance, that thicker, less even veneers and thicker drawer linings are from the pre-Victorian period when these things were cut by hand, and to say that these are better would, more or less, be true; but what about the wonderful, exhibition-quality furniture of the Victorian age, parts of which were cut by machine?

Equally, I could say that early, hand-cut inlays are not as perfect as later machine-cut ones, so you can always judge an older piece by the less-than-snug fit of the inlays, which give a Queen Anne piece its early charm. But I would not always be right, because some very poor-quality country pieces could equally well have poorly fitting inlaid work. I can't tell you to look out for a rich colour, or a pale colour, or a chestnut or a gold, because colour depends on the wood used, and colours can be faked.

I can only tell you that the only way you will learn is by going out and about and using your eyes and your hands. *Look, touch, inspect.* Then ask questions. I cannot stress this enough. It was how I learned.

You will be surprised at how quickly you will start to recognize quality – and conversely, poor quality. Getting your eye in so that you know what it is that you are looking at is not some magic trick: it's probably what you do at home or at work every day of your life, and I can guarantee that you do it when shopping for fruit and vegetables.

Standing right

Like me, you might start off collecting jam pans or a little country chair. Whatever it is, it arouses your curiosity. What is it? What was it used for? Where did it come from? Who did it live with? Old objects have a fascination and nostalgia about them; and as you learn about them you tend to hone your tastes. And the more you know about the craftsmanship and the skill of the designers, the more you start to see what they saw. There is a lot of new terminology to absorb in buying antiques, but it's not the words that matter, so much as what they imply or mean. You hear people say, 'Well that stands very well,' but what does that mean? It means that when the man designed that bookcase, perhaps without even a piece of paper or a pencil, he instinctively knew what looked right because he had years of experience of understanding about balance, style and proportion.

If you see something and you instinctively think, 'It looks a bit dumpy – I wonder why?' it's probably because it was never meant to look like that. It's been cut down, for instance, and has lost its legs. All good furniture has a certain line to it, a certain look, and you'll acquire that appreciation. The more you see, the more examples you study, the more you'll recognize it. I recognize it without even thinking. When I walk into a preview at an auction, if I see a table and my immediate thoughts are, 'It's too low,' it's because it *is* too low. I know it's been cut down. It doesn't stand right and I know it doesn't. Years of experience have taught me this, because I've seen over 300 examples.

It's not as easy when you don't have the experience; that comes with time. But there are good tips:

● **Have** A REALLY GOOD LOOK. Go all the way round it, move it around, pull the drawers out. Ask permission if you're in a shop: 'May I look?' What you're looking for is anything that doesn't look right to you, even if your experience is limited.

● **When** YOU SEE SOMETHING THAT DOESN'T LOOK RIGHT, ASK WHAT IS WRONG ABOUT IT. Don't worry that it'll be impolite to do so: you won't offend anyone. Say something like: 'This seems very low, has it been cut down?' Any dealer worth his salt will tell you more about it at once, and will explain the ins and outs of what you are looking at.

At the end of the discussion you will leave that shop or that stand feeling quite chuffed because one thing you will have learned about yourself is that you can trust your eye and your judgement. You do have a sense of proportion and style.

Asking questions

When you find your examples, where you *can* touch them, don't be shy about looking. Be polite: don't start hauling things around without first asking permission. Then ask questions. Ask the people who are selling. I cannot stress this enough. It was how I learned.

Be honest: never pretend knowledge you don't have, because it will be obvious as soon as you open your mouth. In any case, you want to learn from an expert, so there's no point in getting his back up by trying to impress him – let *him* impress *you*. Say to the dealer on the stand or the owner of the shop, 'I'm looking to buy a spoon-backed chair. I know very little about this. Please can you help me and advise me, telling me all you can about this.'

A lot of people are nervous about following this advice. They are scared of being a nuisance, or of looking silly. But there is an easy way of going about it. Politeness is a great winding sheet. 'Would you do this – could you show me that, could you turn it upside down? I don't know what I'm looking for yet, but I'm hoping you'll show me what you have. I want to have a really good look at this chair.' If you charm the dealer, he is more than likely to let you have a jolly good look and point out a few faults if there are any and offer you advice.

THE SÈVRES VASES

DURING those early years of my gradually developing interest in antiques, I was also accompanying my wife Lorne, who is an international cabaret star, to many exotic locations around the world, where she was booked to appear in various theatres. The shows were usually late in the evening, so during the day we'd have time on our hands. Not keen on sitting around a hotel swimming pool all day, we would go out into the streets and explore the town.

IN HONG KONG, for example, where Lorne would usually be booked for a month at a time, we had plenty of time to get to know the place: we used to joke that we could draw an Ordnance Survey map of the place because we knew every street and every shop. We would buy small, modern items, such as tablecloths, table napkins and china for our dining room; and as our interest grew and developed, we also bought decorative antiques, portable pieces that we could carry home easily in our luggage on the plane, such as small boxes and porcelain. When Lorne performed closer to home, in Europe, we would usually drive and as in those days we had an E-type Jaguar with a tiny boot space, many were the times when we returned home with some treasure precariously strapped to the roof rack.

AROUND 1979, when I was about to open a shop in Wilmslow in partnership with Chris Haworth, a boyhood friend (see page 62), on our travels I spotted a huge French Sèvres porcelain vase with gilt-bronze fittings on a pedestal in an antiques shop in Barcelona. The vase was about 2.5m (6½ft) tall and the pedestal was almost a metre; the two together were quite imposing. I had been in business for a little while and at one of the various sales I attended, I had seen a pair of vases similar to this one, but not as grand and without pedestals, sell for about £25,000, so I felt a wave of excitement that I kept admirably under control as I entered the shop.

I SAID to the owner, 'I like that vase in the window, it's a pity you don't have a pair.'

'OH, BUT I do have a pair,' the owner said, taking me out to the back, and there was another identical vase and pedestal. I knew that this particular pattern of vase was rarely found with matching pedestal, in fact, I had never seen one with a pedestal before; so now I felt a faint flicker of doubt. Were they authentic? The shop owner had bought them privately from a family, a strong point in their favour since such items are known in the trade as 'fresh' or 'unspoilt goods', and, joy of joys, he even had the original invoice from when the family had first acquired them.

'HOW MUCH do you want for these?' I asked. He wrote down in pesetas a figure with a long row of noughts. I did some calculation and to my shock saw that it came to about £130,000. 'This can't be right!' I said. He took another look, scratched his head, saw he'd written one nought too many and knocked it off. The figure now came to £13,000 for the pair. As soon as he said that, even with my limited experience, I knew they were cheap. Now I had to make sure they were genuine and not some modern reproduction.

I CRAWLED all over them, first of all noting that the decorator had signed both vases and pedestals, a sure sign of quality. I particularly looked for genuine signs of age. It is not easy to explain exactly what 'age' looks like, especially with porcelain which can easily be washed. With furniture you have cracks and crannies and wood grain where dirt and polish accumulate. There are corners and fittings such as hinges and handles and carvings that trap more dirt. There is a colour change where sunlight has faded one side or another, and you will often see a difference in colour underneath handles. Drawers that have been slid in and out over a couple of hundred years will be worn in a way that really is quite impossible to fake.

IN THE CASE of these Sèvres vases, I concentrated on what I called the muck of ages that was trapped in and under the ormolu (gilded bronze) mounts. You might think that dirt is dirt, but old dirt has a depth and character to it. It is somehow harder and greasier than new dirt that has just been slapped on to look old. In my opinion, these mounts hadn't been taken off in a hundred years. I lifted the vases and peered underneath, noting old cobwebs, and cobwebs are impossible to fake.

I WROTE DOWN the signature and the factory marks and went back to my hotel, from where I called Chris, giving him the details. He checked them out, by ringing various sources, such as museums and auction houses, and discovered

that the decorator worked in the Sèvres factory in the 1880s. All seemed well.

THERE COMES a stage where you have to make a decision, and sometimes you have to be bold. You have to use your gut instinct even when your knowledge doesn't match. It is my experience that nine times out of ten when in doubt, your instinct will point the way, that and good common sense. You have to think hard and deep and if you want to win you have to have the courage or flair to go forward. This is the case not just with these vases, which were a huge investment for us, but with any big buy you are contemplating making. Sometimes, these decisions are going to be the right ones and everyone's going to be smiling; and sometimes they are going to be wrong ones and there are going to be tears. Unfortunately, learning can be painful experience. But the one thing you can't do if you want to progress is sit on the fence.

WE DISCUSSED the purchase and Chris and I agreed that these magnificent dark blue and gold vases would make a spectacular statement in the window of our new shop. The next day, I went back to the shop, took myself by the scruff of my neck and negotiated, and bought the vases for, I think, £10,000. I had this pair of beauties carefully shipped home with full insurance. After all, ten grand for a young man just starting out in business then was a great deal of money.

THE VASES duly went into the shop window as a showpiece and they seemed to attract considerable attention. About three or four days later, I got a phone call from an Iranian based in London, who was at that time one of the biggest dealers in 19th-century art. 'David, what about the vases?' he said without any preamble.

'OH YES?' I said, realizing that a 'runner' (someone who is paid to seek out items for dealers) must have spotted them for him.

'HOW MUCH are they?' he asked.

'I DON'T want to sell them,' I said. 'I want to keep them as a showpiece for the new shop.'

'COME ON, David, you must want to sell them,' he urged, obviously thinking I was playing hard to get. Now this man had wonderful connections, selling articles to all the sheikhs and princes in the Middle East; a millionaire in his own right, he had homes all around England and Europe. He hadn't achieved that by giving in easily. We argued back and forth with him insisting that I should sell the vases to him and me insisting that I wanted to keep them.

FINALLY, I said, 'Look, I don't want to sell them, but if I ever do, I would want £30,000 from the trade.'

'OH, RIDICULOUS!' he said.

'THAT'S MY PRICE,' I said.

'SEE YOU this evening!' he replied, and put the phone down.

THAT EVENING the dealer and his brother turned up at the shop and walked in, past the 3.5m (9ft) vases as if they hadn't spotted them. 'Well, where are they?' he asked. Of course, it was all part of the game. Then it was, 'Oh, what a shame, they're dark blue, we wanted pale blue.' And so it went, all through dinner and late into the night.

NOW I LOVE the hustle and bustle of the market-place and I was fully prepared not to blink first. But, to cut a long story short, no deal was struck and sometime after midnight we took the would-be buyers to catch the milk train out of Stockport. It was bitterly cold and three or four tramps were bedding down for the night in the warmth of the station waiting room. The train was drawing in when the dealer finally gave in. 'Come on, man, how much will you take?' At the figure I mentioned, the tramps' heads swivelled around. But the deal was struck, and, not much more than a week after I had bought them, I had sold my Spanish finds at the price I wanted. Not bad for a relative novice in the business.

SO THE MORAL of the story? *Do your homework.* Whether you're thinking of spending £10,000 for Sèvres vases or £200 for a dining chair, check them out first in books, with knowledgeable friends, and with the big auction houses.

The Antiques Buyer

Decorativeness

There is one other thing to take into account when you are discussing antiques. Decorativeness is a big word that's very important. Over the last twenty years antiques have gone into a decorative period, and decorative pieces are part of a trend of very desirable, commercial goods. I'm not talking about a frilly-edged table or a commode with lots of ornamentation on it; I mean smaller pieces such as mirrors or vases or lamps or candle holders that are used to decorate your home. One of the reasons for this trend is that although a fairly plain look (bare boards, simple lines and lots of solid colours) is the trend, especially with warehouse and loft conversions, interior decorators are using some very exotic pieces to decorate homes with. You just have to check out *Homes and Gardens* to see what I mean. Magazines like this, as well as the many lifestyle television programmes that show you how to redecorate a room or your home, play a large factor in sparking people's imagination. As a result things that are not in use today have suddenly become fashionable, such as the lacquered screens that were used in the 18th century to stop drafts, which are now used as part of a decoration scheme in a room. The decorative side of a giltwood stand is very appealing and helps create the ambience within a room. It doesn't have a great functional use; you don't sit at it and eat your dinner off it. A lacquer cabinet is another decorative ideal. Open the front of one and you'll discover a series of twelve or more drawers where you could put some small treasures. In the 18th century they put collections of strange and rare tiny things in those drawers to astonish and entertain their guests. A cabinet is an attractive decorative object that can be part of the look that you've created, going hand in glove with everything else, and the ambience you've created.

Sculptures in various stones and metals are also available as decorative pieces, both for inside the home and for outside, for gardens and patios. Generally speaking, these, particularly those by named sculptors, can cost a great deal. But there are a few, perhaps made in spelter (a cheap-grade metal) that are affordable and well worth hunting out. As well as the screens mentioned above there are many more strange and fascinating antique objects that were made to fulfil certain tasks for which they are no longer needed but which make attractive and unusual objects to decorate your home – articles such as telescopes, kitchenalia, machinery, terrestrial and celestial globes, musical boxes and so on – once, I even sold a pair of fairground scales. When it comes to making use of 'different' things, the sky's the limit, so be aware of the decorative value of an antique.

A silk purse or a sow's ear?

Once you've seen something that appeals to your eye, how do you safeguard yourself? How can you tell that it is what it seems to be, that it's not a fake that it or has not been dramatically altered?

A *RESTORATION*, however poor or extreme it might be is essentially a repair job on a piece of furniture or a decorative object. It is not done to deceive, although often the extent of the restoration might well deceive, especially if it is carefully done. It won't fool an expert of course, but it will almost certainly fool a novice. (For more on restoration, see Chapter 5).

A *REPRODUCTION* is a copy of an original piece. It is made in such an honest way that you can tell it is new and the intention is not to deceive the buyer. It can be quite expensive and often very attractive, even if it doesn't have the style and the quality of an original piece. In fact, you can buy such things as 'Chippendale-style' furniture as copies of the original 19th-century pieces. These reproductions or copies have become valuable antiques in their own right.

A *FAKE*, on the other hand, is something that is deliberately created to deceive. It is a pastiche of an older piece, but unlike a straightforward reproduction, it is 'distressed'; that is, it is banged and battered and discoloured to create an aged look. Sometimes fake worm holes are drilled in. (You can tell that they are fake because worms come out at an angle and a drill just goes in straight.) Stains, such as ink and wine are added. If it is a writing desk, a piece of old leather might be used to help pull the wool over the buyer's eye. Some fakes are very cleverly done; but most fakes usually fall down because of the poor quality of materials and workmanship. You should always be aware that they exist and, to avoid being caught with no redress, if buying through a dealer, ask for a signed receipt. If you are fooled at an auction, there is very little redress. (See pages 43–45 for tips on what to look out for.)

THE AUBREY

At a sale of oak country furniture that included some very early pieces, my heart nearly jumped out of my chest when I spotted an Aubrey, an extremely rare Gothic food cupboard. If genuine, it would have been worth £50,000 and in the V & A museum. But I knew it was a fake or, charitably, a reproduction. I checked the catalogue, which stated clearly that this was 20th century, with an estimate of £3000–£4000. This piece was indeed a decorator's item, made to deceive. How did I know? There were a few points that gave it away. The legs had been trimmed and broken to give the appearance of hundreds of years of wear and tear, but the look wasn't quite right – you could see the rounded shape of the ball-pein hammer they'd used to hit it. The strapwork looked old and distressed, but the edges were too straight where they had been machine cut; if it had been hand-beaten all the edges would be spread and flattened with the beating. However, if it had not been correctly identified in the catalogue this piece might have fooled someone less experienced than me.

When you are first starting to buy antiques of course you won't have the experience to tell if something is wrong. You will be surprised at how much you do know, just from instinct and using your eye. But fakers, particularly of paintings, where the stakes are very high, can be very skilful and even experts can be fooled. Easy to spot are new furniture and objects that have obviously been 'distressed', randomly banged about with a chain or a hammer that simply don't have the signs of natural wear and tear. You've only got to compare that look with genuine wear. With a writing desk, for example, you'll see signs of wear on the leather, with the centre more worn where papers, hands and pens have taken the bulk of the wear. On tables and chairs legs are kicked in a certain way over a couple of centuries. On cupboard doors or drawers knobs or handles are worn and rubbed. Not everything shows wear, though. Sometimes I have opened drawers in an apparently old cabinet that look so fresh inside my first instinct was to think the cabinet must be new and therefore a fake. In reality, the drawers have never been used. The piece of furniture, especially if it came from some great house with 365 rooms like Blenheim, might have had a cosseted life sitting quietly for two hundred years in a room that was rarely used. The housemaids would have flicked a duster over it from time to time, but otherwise the skirmishes and knocks of everyday life in a busier room might have passed it by.

Although you should keep a look-out for fakes, I do want to stress that faking antiques is not at all common. Today, while 'crackled' and 'distressed' pine furniture is relatively easy to achieve, it is very difficult and costly to make a determined attempt to fake a good-quality mahogany or marquetry piece because, as I have said, the materials and workmanship don't exist – or if they do, they are very expensive. Faking to a high standard simply isn't worth a counterfeiter's time and pocket.

Generally, what you might more often find is that a badly damaged piece has been extensively – and often poorly – restored and that fact is not mentioned. Or you might find that it is not revealed that a piece has been cut down, for instance, to make them fit into a smaller space, broken up and reassembled with a non-matching part, or altered to suit changing fashion.

If you ask questions, and get a condition report and a signed receipt, you are essentially legally protected and can get your money back, should what you bought prove to have been a fake.

Antiques of the future?

There is an exception to the 'quality, quality, quality' rule and that's in the area of what might be termed 'antiques of the future'. By that, I mean objects that in time will become valuable enough to collect. Often the fact that something is enough to give it a cachet and a value (officially an antique is anything over 100 years old) but today, quality antiques are in such short supply in the market-place and their cost so high that more recent pieces are now being collected. Unfortunately, we don't have crystal balls and can't always tell what are going to be antiques of the future.

With furniture, I don't believe there are many people around today with the necessary degree of skill, training and dedication to make great pieces in the way that they did in the 18th and 19th centuries, when craftsmen worked virtually from the cradle to the grave, seven days a week, turning out great classical designs of great quality. There were people making furniture in England in the 1930s that has already become antiques of the future. By the 1950s and 1960s there were interesting, quirky designs that are now established as important. And there are certain Continental designers making contemporary chairs that are now considered modern masterpieces. But none of these do anything for me and if I applied the quality principle I wouldn't buy any of them. However, it may be that regardless of their quality some will stand the test of time and become true antiques of tomorrow; but whether they will or not is difficult to know.

Some people collect quite modern things, including what is termed ephemera (which are disposable items, or easily breakable objects like boxed games, toys, magazines or comics). In this area I would say look for rarity. If there's only one of something it can fetch an incredible price and obviously, quality becomes secondary. But still we come back to quality as well: *buy mint examples* in the original box. Ephemera is worth nothing unless in its original, unused, pristine condition. It's no good having those with the paper torn off and boxes gone. I'm still not that convinced that mass produced items are good, interesting, yes, but 'good' is not the right word to use. You might say, 'I've got a Barbie doll, that survived above all others, and it's the only pink-haired Barbie in existence.' But it's still a pink-haired plastic Barbie. It doesn't have that element of craftsmanship – found, for instance, in a wonderful, tin-plate toy made in Germany in the pre-war period – which I personally think is important.

When you know what you like, you've got your eye in and money is burning a hole in your pocket, it's time to start making an antique buyer of you.

DAVID'S TOP TIPS

Remember – I may be talking furniture here but most of these tips apply to any antiques.

- *Quality pays.* Try and find the cleanest most honest example of what you want to buy. It's going to cost you a little bit more than the tatty example but in the long run, you will be glad.

- *Buy what you like* – pay no more than you feel you can afford.

- *Ask for the very best price.* Dealers want to do business. Try to negotiate – always ask them what their very best price is.

- *Never over-restore.* Remember, there are degrees of restoration. You can enhance something by restoring it; but, equally, there is a time when you can over-restore and ruin it. If you obey the rule of never buying tat, you won't have this problem.

- With chairs and sofas, *save original covers if you can*, but if they're gone, replace them. No one expects you to sit on stained, worn out rags.

- *Never buy a smiling table.* (Also called yawning tables in the trade.) This is any table with a folding top, such as a card or a games table, a dressing table, a tea table or a sewing box, where the top leaf has warped and no longer sits flat.

- *Highly distressed pieces will distress you.* Avoid them at all costs.

- *Inspection, inspection, inspection, is the name of the game.* At an auction, the goods are on view for perhaps two days. You can go back as many times as you want. Sit back, stand back, weigh it up think about it, measure it up, go home, have a think about it, bring someone else to have a look. You've got plenty of time. Have a good look.

- *Don't be intimidated; inspect everything thoroughly.* Put your hands on it. Open it up and look inside, look underneath, take out the drawers, look behind. Check signatures, hallmarks, stamp marks. Then get advice.

- *Ask questions.* People won't volunteer information unless you ask them. Generally speaking, they won't tell you lies. Seek as much advice from an expert as you can. Sometimes it's worth paying for that advice – it can save you money in the long run.

- *Study a catalogue carefully.* Read between the lines (what does 'decoration refreshed' really mean?). Always read the small print at the back.

- *Buyer beware* – you, and you alone, are responsible for your mistakes.

- *Get a condition report.* This can be either written or verbal.

- *Get a signed receipt or bill of sale.* Remember that the Trades Description Act is there to protect you.

The Antiques Buyer

● *Remember the hidden costs at an auction* – VAT, the buyer's premium and transport home for large items.

● *Be cautious about buying controversial items*, such as lizard-skin suitcases, particularly the ones with a whole head on the top. Even if it's something that's unfashionable at the moment and so you can buy it cheaply, can you use it? Can you sell it? Remember that in the case of something made of animal skin you could end up angering the animal rights people or conservationsists.

● *A painted job can hide a hundred sins.* Gilded, lacquered or painted pieces might not be what they seem. Have a look at the quality of the decoration and inspect the carcass inside. The same is true of any painted piece.

● *Coffee tables are a modern invention.* So-called 'antique' ones are almost always old taller tables that have been cut down, or a top has been put on a brand-new base. If it is a marble specimen table, have a careful look at the base – are those stone dolphins old, or are they modern cement? A lot of these are now flooding in from India – made only last week.

● *How do you tell the difference between platinum and stainless steel,* apart from hallmark if you are buying a collector's watch? Check the weight – platinum is very heavy.

● *Always preview the day before at an auction.* Never bid for anything that you have not thoroughly inspected.

● *Always go to a preview in person* – never rely on the catalogue description.

● *Don't get auction fever.* Know your limit and stick to it, but don't lose it for a bid.

● *Never rush to buy.* If the object you are thinking of buying is at an auction, go to the viewing, go away, come back and have another look and see if you still like it enough to bid. If the object you like is in an antiques shop, sleep on it. See how it feels to the refreshed eye. If it is at a fair, go for a stroll, have a cup of coffee and come back before making up your mind.

● *Always check the outbuildings at a big country house sale.* Bargains are often to be found in dark corners away from the madding crowd.

● *Remember that a local connection can send the price up.*

● *Don't be pressurised.* Avoid the Auntie Wainwrights like the plague.

● *It's in the quality as well as the age.* Appreciate that there is a difference between antiques and second-hand goods.

● *Is it too perfect?* Pristine things are not always what they seem. The chances are they have been very heavily restored, are a fake or a modern copy.

● *Don't buy cracked or repaired ceramics.*

● *Not all antiques are good.* Learn to tell the difference between a trade turn-out or discard and a nice honest piece, fresh to the marketplace.

● *What's underneath that cloth or that brass lamp?* Always lift off an artistically arranged object on top of a piece of furniture you want to buy – it could be hiding a lot of damage, though a little bit of fading is all right. Bubbles in veneer are expensive to iron down.

● *Be ruthless – when in doubt, leave it out.* Some things have had a very tough old life and are only fit for the rubbish bin.

● *Don't buy a worn-out carpet.* At a sale always stay for the turning of the carpets to see what is on the bottom of the pile.

● *Trust your eye.* Buy what you believe in. I have the confidence to do that from years of buying and selling items. Leave room for the unexpected. Always be flexible. Let your eyes and your heart tell you when sometimes you are not sure. Or if acquiring an item means more than the price, if it's special to you, if you've fallen in love with it – buy it.

● *Familiarize yourself with the market-place.* Values and prices change according to the mood and market. A couple of years ago the more decorative items fetched high prices and were fiercely contested; today, people are being that much more careful about what they want to buy. You can use this in your favour if you're buying – Oriental carpets, for example, currently are almost ridiculously cheap. If you're selling such items, hang on until the market goes up.

● *Be prepared to travel for something special.* Look in the trade journals for lists of sales.

● *Avoid a marriage, a liquorice allsort and a cut down.* Stay away from something that has been altered. If it is not what it is supposed to be, it is the kiss of death to buy it. Its value is greatly reduced.

● *The estimate in a sales catalogue is not the selling price* – it is only a guideline.

● *If a piece does not reach its reserve and is 'bought in' (see page 182), sometimes you can go along later and try to negotiate to buy it privately.* This is often true of large pieces that have travelled long distances to a sale; the vendor will not always want the expense of transporting them home again (see my piano story page 116).

● *Always ask about the provenance* – that is, the history of a piece. Sometimes, when you've bought a piece, you can even research this yourself, thus adding value to whatever it is you have bought.

● *Use your common-sense.* If it doesn't look right, it probably isn't. The men who designed the best pieces were excellent craftsmen and designers. You might look at a bookcase and think it looks a bit dumpy. It's obvious to an experienced eye that it's been cut down, but even an inexperienced eye has good, instinctive judgement.

● *Get your eye in by looking,* in as many locations where antique items are displayed as you can – museums, sale rooms, antiques shops and fairs. You don't have to buy in order to learn. As you go along learn to make judgements.

● *Recycle what you can't use.* Trade up. Replace with better.

The Antiques Buyer

3

Where and How to Buy

Now we move on to the meat of the matter: actually purchasing a piece. In this chapter I'll cover the places and ways of buying where you can always remain in control of what is happening. When buying privately, whether it be at an antiques shop, market or fair, it is important to inspect carefully the items you are considering buying. Get your eye in, look at them more than once if you feel like it. Don't rush making any decisions. And don't worry, we'll get to auctions in due course. There's a whole world to tell you about those.

We all make mistakes – everybody does – but by telling you where to buy and what to do when you get there, I hope to save you from some of the pain and the heartache that I have gone through and which hit me in the pocket, because, believe you me, I was very naïve when I first started buying antiques. People were usually very patient and helpful, but I can remember, when I first ventured out into the antiques trade, not knowing even how to haggle in a shop.

Many people feel the same way as I did. They will quite happily go to a boot sale, a Sunday street market or a back-street junk shop, where nothing is very expensive and mistakes won't break the bank, but the idea of venturing into a grander antiques shop or a sale room feels like making a leap into the unknown. By telling you exactly what to expect and what to look out for as well as explaining the normal procedures I hope to demystify the process of buying antiques, enabling you to become a confident, successful buyer.

It's when you actually purchase an antique that you have to make a decision about its value. Before we set off, let's look at some general issues about spending your money wisely on antiques. (I'll tell you about points relating to different kinds of sales as we go along.)

Rising value

Buying antiques ultimately comes down to a matter of taste. You shouldn't really look at it from a financial point of view, though that obviously is a consideration both because antiques can be very expensive and because they can also appreciate in value over the years. It is a fact that over the last 25 years investment reward on English furniture has far outstripped that on the Stock Exchange, as the chart on page 48 shows. Appreciating in value is part of the appeal of buying antiques.

Looking at antiques from a financial position, I think there are still some very good buys around, particularly in antique furniture, although prices have risen rapidly in the last few years and will continue to do so. When you consider the quality and time-consuming work that's gone into it you will appreciate why in many ways this furniture is impossible to reproduce today. A lot of the raw material, of the wood being used, the veneers, are impossible to get today. It's a bit like fish: certain types of wood have been fished out. Cuban mahogany, for instance, which was famous in the 18th century and used for English brown mahogany furniture, has virtually disappeared. There are substitutes such as Honduras mahogany, but they're not quite the same. The distinctive markings, the grainings and colours of the Cuban were very special, so obviously it is very difficult to reproduce that type of furniture today with exactly that look. Considerations like this are all reflected in the price of a piece.

Getting the best value

The one thing you can say when you have bought a piece of antique furniture today is that at the very moment that you take it away from the auction room or a dealer, the price you have paid was the market price, including perhaps the dealer's profit that he has charged you. Nevertheless, if you decide to go around the corner and sell it five minutes later, you would still retain quite a large proportion of the investment that you have made in it; you won't have lost a great deal of its value.

In my experience over the last 25 years, because of the rising interest in antiques and the resulting scarcity of quality goods prices are rising. I think I can be quite emphatic and almost guarantee that over the next 10 or 20 years there will be some kind of improvement pricewise in it. That will depend

ANTIQUE PRICES

BEATING THE STOCK MARKET

'Collectors who have put their money into quality antique furniture can be reassured that their investment is continuing to grow,' reported Clare Stewart in *The Times* in March 1999. According to figures published by the Antique Collectors' Club, antique prices rose 5 per cent in 1998, outperforming both the FTSE 500 share index and house prices in the southeast of England. The Antique Collectors Clubs 20-year graph (below) shows that furniture prices rose particularly sharply during the boom years between 1985 and 1991, and have been rising again since 1995, achieving a substantial gain over the 'Mars Bar' index of consumer price inflation. The highest recent increases have been seen in fashionable oak furniture, usually from the 17th century, which rose by more than 9 per cent in 1998. Edwardian Sheraton-style pieces are very sought after, and mahogany pieces from the 1760s to the early 19th century were also strong in 1998, with a rise of 7.7 per cent.

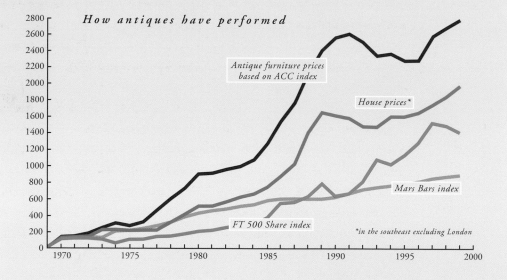

How antiques have performed

Antique furniture prices based on ACC index

House prices*

Mars Bars index

FT 500 Share index

*in the southeast excluding London

very much on trends, fads and fashions: some things have become much more fashionable than other things, while undoubtedly, some things go out of fashion, such as Oriental carpets.

Whether you are hoping to make a profit or simply want to ensure that what you buy doesn't suffer any decrease in value, to be sure of getting good value I suggest you heed the following tips and points.

● **Do your homework**. TAKE ADVICE, talk to experts and look at two or three similar pieces – after doing all the groundwork discussed in Chapter 2, you will be better able to assess prices. Those who jump in at the deep end with a pocket full of money get more than their feet wet. Remember those Sèvres vases (see page 35).

● **Always buy the best you can afford.** DECIDE WHAT YOU CAN AFFORD, buy the best within that price-range – and stick to it. This applies particularly to collectors. I always think that there's not much point to a collection of tat unless you're a rag-and-bone merchant or a pack-rat. Remember also that you don't have to fill your house, garden and garage. Some collectors continually buy and sell, trading up, so that they end up with a collection of just a few of the best examples, having learned about the items in the process.

If you obey these rules, ten or twenty years down the road your little treasure could also turn out to be your golden goose. *Quality* is the key – as I shall keep banging on in this book, quality (see page 23) will always (barring fads and fashions) increase in value. Whatever you're going out to buy try to buy a really good example.

Take two Worcester cups and saucers, for example. Perhaps one has lived in someone's china cabinet all its life; it is unrubbed, the enamel work is in pristine condition and there are no chips or cracks. It has not been handled, there is no general wear and tear, and it is in superb condition, virtually as the day it was made. Then perhaps in the same sale or shop there is another identical example, at least where model and style are concerned, but there the similarity ends. This second cup and saucer has been used frequently over the past century and a half. It has been washed, it has been rubbed. Perhaps there's a little bit of a chip in the cup, a little bit of a crack in the saucer.

Now the difference between the two when it comes to the price on the day of sale will be considerable – because one is a perfect example and the other is damaged goods. It is rare for things have survived in such wonderful condition for such a long period, and the pristine cup and saucer are the ones to go for, even if they are ten times more costly because, in my experience, ten years from now the rising value of the mint example will probably have accelerated. From its current price it might have gone up 400 per cent, whereas the value of the cracked example will have gone up, but might have only moved 50 per cent. Not only that; the aesthetic qualities are much better in a good example.

● **Use your common sense**. ONCE YOU'VE SATISFIED YOURSELF A PIECE IS GENUINE and decided you want it, you need to apply common sense. Common sense tells you that a shop in Bond Street will nearly always charge more than a shop in the back streets of Birmingham. But common sense will also tell you that an expensive shop would soon go out of business if they were wildly overpriced and didn't give good value for money.

Say you are comparing one shop on the corner at Portobello Market and one in fashionable Chelsea. It doesn't take too much thinking to work out that the Chelsea shop has lovely things in it, but it has reasonably high overheads as well. I wouldn't let something like that deter me because my thinking is, true, the shop in Chelsea will charge that extra amount of money because they've got their rates and so forth but it probably has quite a demanding clientele.

I wouldn't automatically discount the one at the corner of Portobello Market, either, because dealers at the bottom end of the market often find great buys and can afford to sell them on reasonably-priced because their overheads are low. One thing, though, that I would like to stress is that sometimes you can get wonderful deals out of very up-market shops simply because they are used to fine pieces and so do not look on them as out of the ordinary, whereas in a small out-of-the-way shop, that Regency mahogany cabinet might be a real treasure to them, so they will price it high. You weigh up all these considerations when you're making your final decision.

Private purchase

Any good antiques dealer will tell you that number one on the list is a private purchase. This is where a private individual invites you to call at his or her home, with a view to selling you a piece of furniture or an object of art. This doesn't happen so much these days because everybody seems to watch antiques programmes on television and as a result now generally send

IT'S THE SAME with a dealer as for a private person: once in a blue moon things come before your eyes during your collecting or dealing life that you have to have.

IT'S NOT LIKE buying a car. If a 1985 Mercedes comes along with 20,000 miles – quite rare and a low mileage – and you can't afford it right then, you can let it pass because the chances are there are many others out there just like it that you might buy some day. But when a wonderful piece of art or furniture comes along in a pristine condition or a particular style that tugs at your heart strings, you have only one chance to buy it. It's true that you do see many examples of certain things, but sometimes you know that you'll never see an example exactly like that ever again. You've got to have courage in this business; you've got to chance your arm sometimes because you don't always get second chances. Some wonderful things do come before your eyes and, wrongly or rightly, you have to get off that fence. This is when I say *forget the rules*.

I'VE KNOWN people who do outrageous things to acquire an object they have fallen in love with – just as people do outrageous things when they're madly in love. They'll say to me, 'I'll put a deposit on it, I'll find the money somewhere, I'll go and sell something, I'll even sell the wife.' Some people go to extremes to raise money – they'll borrow, get an overdraft, whatever it takes to acquire the object of their dreams. Most of the people I've spoken to in later years for whom this has happened still have their pieces. The real kick – the real thrill – is that they acquired whatever it is almost against all odds. It may be worth a great deal more now in financial terms, which is just an added kudos, but they say to me, 'I love it anyway and I'm never going to sell it, however much it is worth.' It is my experience that in most cases when people fall in love with a rare object it is very personal and it is for life. Their marriages may split up but they remain for ever faithful and passionate about their special antique. If you offered them three times the money you couldn't buy it.

their goods to salerooms; contacting their local antiques dealer is something they used to do. So a rush always goes through me when I hear on the telephone that somebody wishes to sell this or that. I drive to the appointment with happy anticipation and I still get excited when I call at a house to hear the words, 'Oh, Mr Dickinson, we've got this table that's been in the family for 200 years but we're moving house and it's too big for us.'

The item could be almost anything, but the magic words are always 'It's been in the family for...' because then you know that the chances are that you will be looking at a genuine, fresh piece that's been well loved and cared for over many generations. It has never come onto the market and now you've discovered it. It's a little like finding buried treasure.

I'm talking now as an antiques dealer. I'll recognize what I'm looking at and, more importantly, I'll know its worth. I'll tell at a glance whether it's a genuine item, or whether the people are trying to pull the wool over my eyes and have knocked it up out of scrap bits of old wood in the garden shed and cleverly 'antiqued' it – not quite, but you know what I mean! And of course not everyone who is selling a fake knows it. Perhaps the sellers themselves have been fooled when they first bought it and it's my job to break the news to them. Then again, people who have inherited 'Grandma's heirloom table' might not be aware that Grandma bought it brand new in 1935 when she got married. Even so to them, it's an old and treasured piece of family history and in such cases I decline to buy in a graceful way that won't hurt the seller's feelings.

If the piece is genuine, I will make a fair offer: one that will satisfy the seller and will leave me room for a modest profit when I sell it on. Of course, it's up to them whether they accept my offer or not. For all I know, they might be ringing round all the local dealers to find out the worth of their piece, and they might well end up by sending it to be sold in an auction.

The following true story about buying in a private context, gleefully told to me by a dealer who presented it as something to be proud of, angered me considerably, and I'm afraid it doesn't show up dealers in a good light. Fortunately, such happenings are rare, but there is a lesson to this story.

An old lady came into this dealer's shop and said, 'I need £120 to pay my rates. Will you come to my house and buy some furniture?' He went to her cottage, quickly identified about £900 worth of goods, and said to her, 'Well, that's £100. What else have you got?' She took him into her bedroom and he proceeded to identify another £200–£300 worth, for which he gave her £20.

To me, it seems outrageous that the seller has no safeguards when a sale is conducted in a private environment, no recourse against an unscrupulous dealer. I wish I could have advised that lady to put her goods into an auction room, but even she probably didn't have the time to wait; sometimes it can take weeks before an auction comes up, there is no guarantee that your goods will sell on the day and even then you still have to wait to be paid.

The moral? If you're determined to sell in this way, *never tell a dealer how much you need.* Don't let him pick and choose his way through your home, show him just one piece and let him make you an offer. *Get at least two valuations before you make your decision.*

But to get back to buying. What about you, as a private buyer? How do you get to see private pieces? How do you know if the piece you're there to inspect is genuine and how much to offer for it?

First of all you might see an advertisement in a newspaper or a card in a shop window. Usually, the advertisement will tell you basic information such as dimensions, possibly what it is made from (in the case of wood most people know the difference between pine, oak and mahogany) and how much they want for it. Occasionally the advertisement will say 'offers', in other words, the sellers may be as green as you about the value of their piece and are hoping for an offer that will make them sit up.

Get on the telephone and ask for a detailed description of the table: dimensions such as size and height, shape of legs, any carving, if there are drawers (kitchen tables might have drawers; dining tables do not) materials and approximate age. Ask – if the advertisement hasn't said so – how much they want, then make an appointment to view.

If you have the time, before going to the house, pop into as many local antiques shops as possible to inspect similar tables and ask questions. What is that table made from? How much more would it be worth if it had two leaves, or four? What price range do such tables fall into? You can also look in books about antiques (see page 187). Books can only show a few examples; they can never let you get your hands on the object to feel the wood and the values are nearly always out of date or guesstimates. However, a good book can give you a rough idea of the difference between shapes and styles, such as a pedestal leg or a cabriole leg and a claw foot or a pad foot.

When you arrive at the house and they show you the table, the first thing you should do is to measure it, to reassure yourself that it will fit in your dining room. It is amazing the number of people who, when asked for dimensions over the telephone, give a rough estimate that is usually wrong.

You will know at once if this table you're now looking at 'looks right'. If it has a table cloth and ornaments on it, ask the seller to take everything off so

Buying from a friend

ONE RATHER DIFFICULT AREA I am often asked about is what you should do if you are buying an antique from a relative or a good friend. You want to be scrupulously fair and the piece is valuable, but how do you go about it? First, you should ask for a valuation from a dealer and stick to that price. It will cost you a few pounds in the valuer's fee but will save any possible bad feeling later. You should also ask the valuer to give a condition report (see page 89) and attach this to your receipt, which the vendor should sign. You might say you don't need a receipt between friends, but where money is concerned, you should always be business-like; and it is certainly a useful document for all the reasons I've given above, regardless of whether the vendor is a friend or not.

that you can have a proper look. If it is stuck in a corner of the hall where there is no light, ask if you can carry it into a room with a better light. Then remembering what I've said about common sense and using your eyes, not to mention your very fresh look at a few genuine antique tables, see if the table still looks right. Get on your hands and knees, and look under the table. Tip it over if it's light enough and look at the colour of the carcass. Does it look raw and new? Are there shiny new screws? Are there brackets holding the legs on (a sure sign of serious structural damage)? Can you see where new stain has been slapped on, indicating that the piece is fake or has been extensively rebuilt?

If all looks well to your sensible, albeit untrained eye, discuss the price. You should have some idea of what this size and type of table will be worth because of your initial research. At this stage you might well fall into a moral dilemma. Suppose similar tables you have seen in antiques shops cost anything up to £6,000 and these people naïvely are asking just £150: what should you do? In my case, as a dealer, I am usually called in to make an offer or to value goods, so I have a professional duty to be fair and a reputation to maintain; but a private buyer does not have that duty or reputation. I can't tell you what to do – that has to be up to you. Whatever you offer, it is also up to the seller to protect himself. Just as you have taken the trouble to do your homework, he should have done the same. But I would always advise you to be fair. What goes around comes around.

Get a receipt

You want to buy the table and you've agreed a price – but remember that the principle governing the law is 'buyer beware' (see Sale of Goods Act 1979, page 56). 'Buyer beware' is a legal term that means exactly what it says. By law you are responsible for your decision to purchase or not – the risk is on your side. If you're not yet such an expert that you know exactly what it is that you're buying, you can safeguard yourself a little: *always ask for a detailed receipt.*

In the example of your private purchase of a table, ask the owners to write on a piece of paper what they have told you over the telephone or in person. They might not know the style, the date, or the type of wood, but they could say: 'A 3.5m (9ft) table, believed to have been in the family for over 100 years, of a solid reddish-brown wood believed to be mahogany with square legs and three leaves.' Get the owners to date and sign it. If the table proves to be made in 1960 and made of plywood, in principle you have some redress and can ask for your money back. This applies to anything that you buy, whether Clarice Cliff 'Bizarre' pottery, a picture or a sideboard.

An additional reason for asking for a receipt is to prove that you own the antique you have just purchased. If you pay for it by cash without a receipt, and it is amazing the number of things that change hands this way, how can you prove, should the occasion ever arise, that you paid for it? Sometimes antiques have been known to have been stolen; in order to prove that you paid for it, get that receipt. It may also be useful for insurance purposes, when you have to decide how much to value a piece for, your insurance company will require a receipt in the case of a claim.

A receipt – also known as a bill of sale – can also protect you. Under the Trades Description Act you cannot be misled – and if you are, the perpetrator can be guilty of a serious offence. If you were to come to me and say, 'I would like to buy that bookcase, Mr Dickinson, please would you tell me about it?' I'd say, 'Well, it's definitely Continental, possibly Swedish, 19th century, probably *circa* 1890 to 1900 (*circa* meaning 'round about'). It's in good, original condition, with its original, untouched gilding. We've cleaned it. There have been some little knocks and chips so we have done some light restoration to it. I'm prepared to sell it to you for – ' and then we would start to negotiate, after which I would put that agreed price down on your receipt, together with something like: 'In good original condition, *circa* 1890 – Continental – walnut and gilt.'

When you went away you would have something in your hand that would tell you exactly what you had and would be legally binding. If at some stage in the future it turned out not to be what I said it was, if it turned out to be 1950s and was faked to look old or heavily restored, you could come back to me and say, 'This was total misrepresentation. I want my money back.'

The situation is a little different in a saleroom or an auction. There it is very much a case of buyer beware (see page 94).

BUYER'S RIGHTS

The following points should not be taken as the difinitive guide to consumer law. I hope they will give you pointers to what your rights in normal circumstances cover. It doesn't matter if you buy from an individual, a shop, fair, market or auction, these rights still apply. These are your statutory rights and cannot be withdrawn from you by any small print in catalogues or receipts or 'terms of business'

1. GENERAL

It must be emphasised that the buyer can only effectively exercise any available right

a) if he can find the seller after the purchase of any item has been completed; and

b) if the seller is of sufficient financial means to return the purchase price and/or compensate the buyer

This is one very good reason for buying from a reputable dealer. The buyer is most unlikely to be able to trace a seller from a car boot sale.

If buying from an agent e.g. a dealer selling on behalf of a private seller, then any claim will only be against the private seller and not the agent, unless the agent has failed to make clear that he is acting as agent

When buying any item, ask for a receipt which gives the

a) date of purchase;

b) purchase price;

c) full description of the item being purchased; and

d) name and address of the seller

2. IMPLIED INTO AN AGREEMENT WHEN YOU BUY

If the seller is selling privately or in the course of a business

a) That the seller owns what he is selling (a condition). Note that if a stolen item is bought, the buyer will not obtain title to that item. If it is claimed by the original owner, then it will have to be returned to that original owner. The buyer's only recourse is against the seller for the return of the purchase price together with any other foreseeable losses. S.12 (1) Sale of Goods Act 1979

b) (Unless anything is said to the contrary) that the item being bought is free from incumbrances e.g. not subject to any form of finance agreement (a warranty). However, if the item is a vehicle and bought by a private buyer, in good faith, without notice of that finance agreement, then the buyer will obtain the vehicle free of the finance agreement. S.12 (2) Sale of Goods Act 1979 S27 Hire-Purchase Act 1964

c) That the item being bought will correspond with its description (a condition) S.13(1) Sale of Goods Act 1979

If the seller is selling in the course of a business

That the item is of satisfactory quality (a condition). What this means is that a reasonable person would regard it as being of satisfactory quality after taking into account i) the description of the item, ii) its price, iii) its appearance and finish, iv) its freedom from minor defects, v) its safety, vi) its durability, and/or vii) its fitness for the purpose for which an item of the kind in question is commonly supplied. However, a) if what makes the item unsatisfactory is either drawn to the buyer's attention before the contract is made or b) the buyer has a full opportunity to examine and the examination would have revealed the defect, then the buyer cannot claim that that defect makes the item unsatisfactory. S.14(2) Sale of Goods Act 1979

3. MISREPRESENTATIONS

If the buyer is told something by the seller which has the object and result of persuading the buyer to buy the item and what the buyer has been told is false, then the seller has made a misrepresentation. On finding out about the misrepresentation, the buyer has a choice of either rescinding the contract, i.e. giving back the item and recovering the purchase price, or receiving compensation. This applies whether the misrepresentation was made by the seller fraudulently or innocently. Sections 1 and 2 Misrepresentation Act 1967

4. EXCLUDING LIABILITY

As long as the buyer is acting as a private consumer, the seller cannot exclude or restrict his liability.

5. REMEDIES

If the breach is a breach of condition or misrepresentation, the buyer is entitled to his or her money back on return of the item together with any other foreseeable loss, e.g. travel costs. If the breach is a breach of warranty, then normally the only entitlement is to compensation for the loss suffered, e.g. if the item is subject to a finance agreement, then the cost of paying off that finance agreement.

6. ENFORCING THE REMEDY

If the seller will not voluntarily compensate the buyer or take back the item, then the only remedy might be to take court proceedings against the seller. Before doing this the buyer must give the seller every opportunity to compensate the buyer for his or her loss. The buyer should write to the seller, keeping a copy of the letter, setting out why he has a claim, what is wrong with the item and what the buyer wants, e.g. money back. If the buyer has any document supplied by the seller on making the purchase (e.g. the receipt referred to above), then he should send a copy. If the buyer has been told by an expert that the description of the item is not correct, then that should be embodied in a written report and a copy sent to the seller. The buyer should make clear what he is looking for by way of compensation and that the letter will be referred to at any court hearing on the question of costs. Legal advice should be considered if the loss is likely to be substantial.

THE PEACOCK

IN ABOUT 1983 I purchased two magnificent Minton majolica vases (shown on this page). In order to research the history of these two huge pieces, I went to the wonderful Minton museum at Stoke-on-Trent, Staffordshire, where I met the charming curator, Joan Jones, who has written several books on Minton ware. She identified my two vases at once as being of the Bacchus design and she showed me the one in the museum. She asked me what I would be doing with my two examples, and I said, 'I will offer them for sale, possibly at one of the big antiques fairs.' Very helpfully, she said, 'Look, there's an avid American collector who often comes to the museum. I'm sure he would want to look at your vases. I'll put you in touch with him.'

I MET HIM and he bought the vases. I also advised him to buy a pair of wonderful Minton blackamoors he had been offered elsewhere for the then enormous sum of £36,000. 'In my opinion they are the finest Minton pieces you will ever see,' I told him. 'You will never regret it, and their value will increase substantially.' He took my advice and bought the blackamoors, and I started looking out for unusual and rare Minton pieces for him. He told me that what he really craved was a Minton peacock. Known as one of the most potent images of the 19th century, the peacocks were modelled by a famous sculptor, Paul Comolera, round about 1873. It is thought that there are only twelve examples remaining, one was in the Minton museum, but none had

ever turned up for auction at that time (around 1983). Rather rashly, I said, 'I am sure I can find you one. Leave it to me.'

I DID SOME more research and found several letters written over the years by people who actually owned one of these peacocks and who were seeking verification of what they had or checking details of its history. One letter was written from a Derbyshire hotel, the Peacock View I think. It was reasonably close by, so I jumped into my car and off I went to the hotel. As I approached the hotel my heart leaped into my mouth when I saw the peacock looking at me from the top of a stone wall. I was astounded that such a valuable object was perched in such a vulnerable position. But when I got out of my car and saw that it had been broken from its original base and was concreted on to the wall. I turned around and drove home.

A SECOND letter that was several years old was from a woman who owned a hotel on the Isle of Wight. Spontaneously, without pause to think things through, again I jumped in my car and, after a ten-hour journey, I arrived at the Peacock Vane Hotel.

I WALKED into the lobby, and nearly fainted. Staring at me from its position in the corner was a magnificent 2m (7ft)-high peacock: a Minton majolica bird, a highly glazed earthenware figure, standing on its rock in all its glory. It was perfect. The first time you are confronted with one of these peacocks is a quite sensational experience because, rarity apart, the peacocks are so imposing and very beautiful. Even though I had seen one before, I got so excited that I had to go outside, just to calm myself down. Then I came back inside and asked for the owner.

HE TURNED OUT to be the son of the woman who had written the letter, who had since died. I told him that I represented an American collector and that I had been searching for this one piece, which had eluded him for some time. 'Will you sell it?' I asked.

'NO,' he said.

'BUT I HAVEN'T even offered you a price,' I said, reeling from this flat refusal.

HE SAID, 'I wouldn't sell at any price,' and walked away, back into his office, having given me less than three minutes of his time and leaving me with a depressing ten-hour return journey home, empty-handed.

TO SAY that I was disheartened was an understatement. But now I was even more determined to find another peacock. Amongst the letters I had was one from a woman who lived in Sydney, Australia. I wasn't going to rush all the way there quite so impetuously. A little research produced a telephone number and I spoke to the woman. That was the start of a lengthy negotiation of the sale of her peacock during which she told me about another peacock. Destined for the 1880 International Exhibition in Melbourne, it had been shipwrecked when the *Loch Ard* went down some 22.5 kilometres (14 miles) off the Australian coast. Still in its crate, the peacock was washed up, intact. Now in the Melbourne Museum it was known as the Loch Ard Peacock and insured for one million Australian dollars.

'IT'S NOT worth that much,' I told her. 'It's a publicity stunt.' In truth, I didn't know how much one of these peacocks was worth, but I knew it wasn't anything like that amount. However, I based my offer for this woman's peacock on some other magnificent birds by the same sculptor, Comolera, such as his far smaller, and more numerous, storks and herons, which were used as stick stands, which sold for round about £3,000.

AFTER much discussion. eventually she agreed that she would sell her peacock to me for £13,000. At once I telephoned my collector at his home in

Long Island and we agreed a price. To the Australian woman I said, 'I'm bringing you a certified bank draft, you won't let me down, will you?' She said that she would not, so I bought a round-the-world ticket and flew out.

IN AUSTRALIA, she told me a remarkable story about her peacock. Before the Second World War her husband had decided to sell it to an Indian maharajah and it was shipped out to India. The war intervened and the bird spent the war crated up on the docks of either Bombay or Calcutta. At any rate, it was never delivered and, somehow, ended up back with her. 'My husband loved it,' she said gazing at it nostalgically. Fearful that she was about to change her mind, I asked the shippers to carry it out of her house and crate it up on the van instead of *in situ* as is usual.

I TELEPHONED the American and told him I had his peacock and was shipping it. It would be with him within a few weeks. 'No, I can't wait, I want it air-freighted out at once,' he said. His brother was to tell me that when the bird arrived, the collector was so excited that he left a multi-million-dollar property negotiation in order to watch it being unpacked at his huge mansion on Long Island. Although we had agreed a price, £25,000, he still haggled, thinking he had me over a barrel. When I pointed out that one of these magnificent objects had never turned up at open auction and I would be glad to offer it for sale at one, he ungraciously paid me the full amount. He went to the extreme length of tracking down the air freighter I had used to ask how much I had declared on the bill of lading from Sydney, on which I had to fill in the price I had paid. When he discovered it was half what I had sold it to him for, he was furious. It had taken over three months' hard work to track down and buy the peacock. My air ticket had cost several thousand pounds, and I had paid for hotels, air freight and insurance, but he didn't acknowledge any of that. Ultimately, I was vindicated in my valuation: in 1998 one sold for £95,000 at Christie's, a dazzling rise in value.

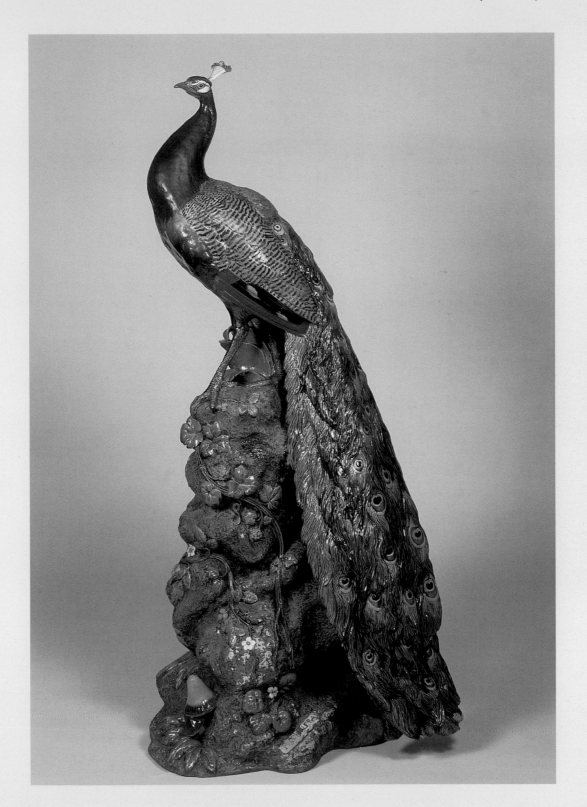

Antiques shops

Much more likely than a private purchase is that you'll buy in an antiques shop. While we're on the subject, let me digress a little and tell you the story of my own.

I had known Chris Haworth since my first day at school. Our friendship continued through into our marriages. Lorne and I and Chris and his wife used to go to each other's homes for dinner or just drop in for a chat. Like me, Chris was interested in antiques and collected a bit, although he didn't buy and sell as I did. One day, out of the blue, when the four of us were together, Chris and I suddenly decided we should have a go at running our own business. It was an enormous step. Chris was making a good living as a fleet car manager for a major automobile company and he'd be giving up the security of that to open up a shop and stock it in the hope that we could attract customers and make it work. But Chris's character complemented mine; we were two sides of one coin. I was the more flamboyant, gregarious type while he was steady and more cautious, working quietly away in the background. Many people have thought I was the more outgoing partner, but we had a partnership of equals. Back then, when we were both so new and green in the business I don't think either of us could have done it without the support of the other.

Encouraged by our wives, we put in about £1,500 each to buy and stock a little shop in the centre of Disley. I was travelling with Lorne at the time as her manager and was home for just a couple of weeks at a time, but Chris ran the business full time. At first, before we could afford an assistant, this was a problem because one of us would have to go out on the road buying, while the other was running the shop.

Simple things we hadn't taken into account, like how to value, how to price up our pieces, were just hit and miss until we became more experienced. We'd take turns to look after the shop and go out on the road, our wives helped with cleaning and dusting – we all pitched in. It was an enormous jump into the unknown, but we didn't think we were doing anything that remarkable. I know that many would-be antiques dealers will be very cheered by my modest beginning – it shows that the sky's the limit if you have confidence.

In fact, we had remarkable confidence. A little back-street junk shop filled with cheap bits and bobs was not for us. We wanted the *best*, right from the start, even if we were stretching our resources to the limit and beyond. We wanted the spotlights in the shop window and Bond Street glamour. Not for us an ad in the local paper – we wanted the glossy advertisement in the best position in a trade magazine, the one the top dealers and collectors subscribed to – and the approach paid off.

One day a Swedish lawyer based in Disley, who used to buy regularly from us, mentioned that he had contacts in Sweden who were very interested in antiques. When he said that he would tell them about our shop and the nice things we had, I don't think we paid much attention. One day the lawyer turned up at the shop with a tiny man, about 1.5 metre (5 feet) tall, dressed in a cowboy's regalia – the Stetson, the shirt, the bolo string tie, the jeans, the cowboy boots. This elf spoke very little English, but speaking through the lawyer he said he was very impressed with the stock. Eventually, after inspecting every piece, he asked, 'How much?'

I said, 'How much for what?'

'All of it!' he replied.

Chris and I were stunned. We just looked at each other, too amazed to speak. Eventually we decided we would simply open up our stock books, show him what every item had cost us and ask for a straight 17.5 per cent profit on top of that. He agreed – and we sold him the whole stock. There were about five or six other antiques shops in Disley and word sped around the village that Dickie and his pal had got a millionaire 'Texan'. Everyone flocked by to get an eyeful of this phenomenon, but he didn't buy from anyone else.

This 'cowboy' turned out to be one of the wealthiest men in Sweden. His name was Bent Erlanson, known to his friends as Little Bent. I didn't know at that stage that he was a multi-millionaire entrepreneur and ombudsman who was fascinated by cowboys, going every year to the Tucson Round-up in Arizona. Apart from many commercial interests he also had a Disneyland type of ranch in Sweden that he had named the Ponderosa, like the TV series. After cleaning us out, he invited us to visit him in Sweden. We went and discovered that the reason he had bought all our antiques was to supply the shops in his Western-style holiday camp environment – a Butlin's for cowboys, with shoot-outs in the street and Wild West shows.

Little Bent came once more to Disley with three other Swedish businessmen, all major players in their own areas: one was the marzipan king of Sweden; another was the burger king of Sweden and the last one was the frozen food king of Sweden. Between them, they bought up the shop again.

Things went so well that eventually Chris and I got up to about £90,000 turnover. In those days there was stock relief, which meant that you could invest your profits without paying tax back into the company. With me having eyes bigger than my belly, it wasn't long before we focused our sights on the Mayfair of Cheshire – Wilmslow. We had warnings from many people that it was all frock and no knickers there, but I wouldn't be told. Selling our shop in Disley at a handsome profit, in 1980 off we went to open a glamorous emporium in the centre of Wilmslow at a hefty rent, since we couldn't find anywhere to buy. But business was never good and a recession was looming. Three years later, Chris and I amicably decided to split up and go in different directions – remaining the best of friends until he died.

After Chris and I closed that business down, I considered opening on my own in Manchester. I did my sums, totted up my capital, and was rather nervous at the high overheads, more than anything I had incurred before. But then I remembered Imad Al-Midani, whom I had first met when he bought some of the finest pieces from the Wilmslow shop. I asked Imad if he would like a silent interest in the business, to which he readily agreed.

Imad was the most generous, gentlemanly person I had ever met. Even though he had been brought up in a fabulously wealthy family, educated at the American School in Beirut and completed his education in England, he was very modest and charming. I remember once when we and our wives went to stay at the Dorchester for the weekend, even though his father was a main shareholder of the Park Lane hotel, Imad was the kind of man who, when we came down for dinner in the evening and the *maitre d'* came rushing across, courteously insisted that we were not given priority over existing customers, but would be seated only when convenient. And even though he was a partner in the business he insisted on paying the full price with mark-up for every piece I sold him to furnish his wonderful country mansion. The business thrived for a few years. But this antiques business is not all go, go, go: things can get very tough. When another recession hit the country seven years later in 1991, at the same time as the tripling of my rent, I decided to dissolve my partnership with Imad and close the shop. I started to concentrate on fair,s something that I had already been doing successfully for some years, and now I make a good living by buying carefully and doing two or three fairs a year.

Buying in an antiques shop means, of course, that you're going to encounter an antiques dealer. Now before you say it, let me say it. Antiques dealers are untrustworthy rogues and sharp practice is the norm – or at least

THE KILLARNEY
STATE COACH LAMPS

I'M NOT SAYING that the Aukin twins were Auntie Wainwright-type dealers, because they weren't, and I did a lot of business with them. But there is no denying that they knew how to sell and they certainly had the gift of the blarney. In their premises even the most astute dealer, including me, could succumb to what I call the junk-shop syndrome. One knows it well: the madness that can overtake you when entering a dusty emporium overflowing with mountains of fascinating and curious stuff. It's like going into an Aladdin's cave, where you know treasure is just waiting to be found.

THE TWINS were like tiny little leprechauns, barely five feet tall, a wonderful, colourful pair of characters, well known in the Dublin furniture trade. Their large warehouse was an ideal port of call whenever I was in Ireland and they had some wonderful things, and, even though they gave the impression that they had no idea what was there in the dusty recesses of the warehouse, they knew where everything was. On one occasion, when I was looking for goods for my first large international fair, I popped in and after spending a few minutes chewing the cud, I asked them if they had anything different.

ONE BROTHER turned to the other and said, 'Perhaps you could show David the Killarney state coach lamps?'

WELL, my ears pricked up at that. I could barely control my excitement. One of the little leprechauns went off down the warehouse and some considerable time later came staggering back under a massive pair of metal lamps that were at least 1.5m (4½ft) high. They were the largest coach lamps I had ever seen, in wonderful condition, every bit intact. By now, as you can imagine, my eyes were glistening, staring out of my head like organ stops.

'THERE YOU ARE, David,' puffed the brother proudly. 'The Killarney state coach lamps!'

OF COURSE I swallowed this implied romantic provenance, hook, line and sinker. Like everyone else who visits the Emerald Isle when confronted with a potent story, I was beguiled into believing it, because I wanted to. And it's true that the lamps were of the quality I expected. So, wanting to get them away from there as quickly as possible before they had second thoughts about them, almost joyfully I paid out the enormously expensive £1,800 asking price. A normal pair of lamps, far smaller of course, would have fetched perhaps a couple of hundred pounds. But these were special, these were the Killarney state coach lamps themselves!

ONLY they weren't. They turned out be hearse lamps. Fortunately, however, they were authentic and rare, and I later sold them at Olympia for a handsome profit.

Carlton Hobbs I'm a great admirer of a very stylish

firm in Pimlico owned by two young men my age: the Hobbs brothers, Carlton and John. To my eyes they are some of the leading lights of the antiques business in this country today. They have risen to the pinnacle by stocking the most exquisite, extraordinary, and expensive items. If you're a highly discerning collector, a Rothschild or a international movie star or an interior decorator who wants to knock a client's socks off, then you'd go there. These are men who in the last 25 years have become prominent because of their eye and ability to acquire the most dramatic and superb pieces. There are several places you would go to in the world for the exotic and extraordinary: a certain dealer in Paris, one in Rome, but when in London it would have to be Carlton Hobbs.

many people seem to think so. I don't agree. It would be naïve of me to say that these individuals don't exist – they do. Like all businesses, it takes all types. Above all avoid the likes of dear old Auntie Wainwright, the shrewd junk-shop owner in the beguiling television series, *The Last of the Summer Wine*. The Auntie Wainwrights of this world have the knack of luring innocent customers into their shops and selling them fools' gold, something they didn't want, often at hugely inflated prices, and before you know it, you're out of their shop, invoiceless and clutching some piece of rubbish.

In fact there are fewer problems, believe it or not, in buying from an established and reputable antiques, inasmuch as you are dealing with someone who has a good reputation to protect and they want to *keep* that good reputation. True, you have to negotiate a price with them and it's up to you to decide if the price is a fair one; but at the end of the day, that dealer has to give you a bill of sale. He has to describe on that piece of paper what he has sold you and, depending on how persistent you are, you can ask for a huge amount of detail to be included. This piece of paper can protect you (see page 54).

But I'm pleased to say, that in my experience, the vast majority are *good* dealers. Over the years I've met and dealt with thousands. They have been a mixture of hard-working professionals and some of the most wonderful characters that one could possibly hope to meet.

Trade societies

Many of the major dealers belong to societies, such as the British Antique Dealers' Association (BADA), which I belong to, or the London and Provincial Antique Dealers' Association (LAPADA), both of which are highly respected. There are many criteria to joining such organizations. First of all, you are invited to join: you don't apply. They have codes of practice and regulate their members as a lot of professional bodies do. Membership of one of these societies is not a 100 per cent guarantee of a dealer's integrity, but a dealer being a member of a society that has rules, regulations and codes of ethics is a good indication. However, I would not want to say that someone who is not a member of a society is not a good dealer, because there are many who choose not to join. I was approached many times to join BADA, recommended by other members, and I did not join immediately. I thought long and hard and finally I did join because it is so well-regarded throughout the world; my feel-

Jack Donovan In Portobello Road there used to be a man with a small shop crammed with the most extraordinary toys, wonderful automatons. One of the biggest collectors of automata in the world was Prince Rainier of Monaco. Jack Donovan was known as the King of Toys. The door to his wonderland was never left open: you'd have to knock. A face would appear, and if he half liked the look of you he'd let you in. (Some of the more eccentric dealers would never let you in. I could never figure out how they did any business.) As a young guy I'd say politely, 'Mr Donovan, please may I come in and have a look at some of your pieces?' He'd show me, talking me through his rare collection. What were toys in the 19th century can go for £50,000 today.

Most of Jack Donovan's collection was not for sale. He'd sell some lesser pieces in order to survive, but he was an example of a dealer who in his heart is a collector, someone who can't bear to let many of his things go. You can still be a dealer and build up a collection by keeping certain things back. I try not to do that, but one day I might wake up and think to myself, 'No, I cannot and will not sell that,' and then I'll know that I have caught the bug.

ings were that being a member would be helpful to give confidence to my international clients. Also, there are many things you can go to the society for, such as legal advice, advice on shipping, regulations and so forth. Both are highly respected. BADA and LAPADA both have their own fairs in London once a year: BADA has the Grosvenor House Fair and the BADA Fair on the King's Road; LAPADA has one at the Royal College of Art in Kensington and also a show at the National Exhibition Centre in Birmingham.

Where are the best dealers?

Many of the best-quality dealers are in London. An example of someone with an eye for the extraordinary is Guinevere in the Kings Road, a French lady who has been there for many years and gained a first-class reputation for decorative antiques. When she first opened her shop in the New Kings Road she was perhaps one of only a few people in what was considered then an unfashionable part of the road; now 50 shops have gathered around her like moths around a flame.

There are of course the establishment firms on Bond Street, such as Partridges for some English but mostly grand Continental furniture; and Mallets, supplier of English furniture in early walnut – very much the absolute top-of-the tree retail house. In Pimlico Road a group of designer quality antiques businesses has grown up with a whole new look – it's stylish and it's hip. The Fulham Road is now a secondary Bond Street in many ways, with a collection of top-drawer English furniture dealers, and Westbourne Grove is getting to be a hub of commercial dealers.

In the country there are many established antiques dynasties, run by the same family for several generations. These demonstrate that the very best of everything is not only to be found in the West End of London: it can also be found elsewhere, in established country firms which have been working for many years in places such as Harrogate and Bath. (In recent years Bath has dried up a little, but nevertheless, it's a great hunting ground with lots of shops). The Cotswolds are perhaps the richest hunting ground in the country, though they are declining a bit from a dealer's point of view. There was a time 15 or 20 years ago when the Cotswolds were at their peak. A lot of travelling dealers from all over the world used to go there; but by and large they've moved on, like a shoal of herrings for new feeding grounds, perhaps leaving more space for the modest private antiques hunters to browse.

Fairs and markets

Many people are wary of this type of bazaar-like venue because they think they're filled with rogues, tinkers and snake-oil charlatans. But such places do have merits and advantages. To me these are the most interesting and the most fun because you never know what you'll find. However, by their very nature, these venues can be quite casual, and, unless you're going to an established and fairly grand fair, such as those at NEC in Birmingham, or at Olympia or the Grosvenor House Hotel in London, where the dealers are carefully vetted, often it really is a case of 'buyer beware': it's all very well getting a nice guarantee or bill of sale, but that's no use to you if the seller does a runner and you never see them again. But there are many different types of venues and some are better than others.

● **Car boot sales.** BOTTOM OF THE PILE are the informal and local car boot sales increasingly being held up and down the country, where you can buy almost anything from second-hand clothes to garden plants. You can also buy the odd genuine antique, and, if you're very lucky, you might even buy a frippery for a couple of pounds that turns out to be Fabergé and worth £10,000. It is the thrill of the unexpected that keeps people going to car boot sales, although for a serious antique hunter looking for a particular item, I would never recommend them since you might have to go to dozens and still not find what you are looking for. The biggest drawback to these smaller markets is that you can buy a load of rubbish on the spur of the moment; the plus side is that nothing ever costs very much so if you later decide you've made a mistake, you won't be too much out of pocket.

● **Open-air or flea markets.** THESE ARE NEXT UP THE SCALE. There are the summer ones, such as those you can find in huge fields, showgrounds or cattle markets, some of which are milestone events in the calendar with several thousand stallholders congregating there to sell their wares. Established flea markets are held regularly, weekly and even daily, such as the one in the centre of Paris.

If you want to branch out and be adventurous on holiday you can find them through guide books or your travel agent, though remember that, whatever you buy, you have to carry back with you. On one occasion when I was quite new to the antiques game, Lorne and I were in Spain, and I spotted a large terracotta figure of a man for sale. It was German and had spent most of its life in a castle high in the Pyrenées. For some reason, I took a fancy to it. We had our small Jaguar E-type and on to the roof rack went this life-size object. Driving it home was quite nerve-racking, as we jolted down mountain roads, over potholes and around sharp bends. At any moment I expected shards of terracotta to shower down around us, but the figure survived and

Be careful when buying at 'flea markets'. Getting redress, if anything is wrong, can be a very difficult task.

arrived home without a crack. Embolded by this, in Italy we bought faience and majolica pieces, in Portugal, earthenware pans and pots – we used to drag back some strange and exotic bits and pieces, all strapped on to that roof rack.

If you are prepared to take a chance that what you are buying is genuine, because I doubt if you'll ever be able to get a refund from a flea market held in a field near Budapest, and you have the space in your luggage or in your car, then you can get some very striking pieces from as far afield as Russia or East Germany, where a new market in antiques has opened wide. In those areas money is in such short supply that many people are having to sell family heirlooms for tragically small sums. If you're lucky, and can overcome the language problem, you can buy historic pieces, such as lost treasures of the Romanov period, or early Communist memorabilia, which are increasingly collectable. However, I cannot put my hand on my heart and say, yes, buy this or that, because those are specialist fields and you need to be an expert to be sure of what you're getting. There are very few books available in English for research and the value of antiques from Russia, Poland and other former Communist countries is still a largely unknown territory.

● Emporiums. THESE ARE PLACES WHERE, AT A SINGLE LOCA-TION, such as a mall or an arcade, a large warehouse or a street market, a permanent group of dealers display their wares. Usually, their space is very small and for that reason most of them specialize in smaller objects, whether furniture, decorative items, silver and jewellery or collector's items, from comics to books to toys. If you are looking for something particular or something to add to your collection in a friendly atmosphere, this is the kind of place to go. For example, in Bermondsey, London, you can find a street market early every Friday morning, jam-packed with stallholders selling the most eclectic range of articles. You will often find 'the trade' here, dealers who perhaps own rather grand shops, looking for bargains. If they can bargain and find good deals so can you, but you must get there early before the tourists arrive. Remember that as these stallholders have to unpack and then pack up everything they don't sell, they'd far rather sell to you than take it all back to the lock-up where they store it. Most major towns have similar markets or emporiums.

It is worth pointing out that because the stall- or booth-holders are permanent or regulars, they are not normally fly-by-nights who will con you, take your money and do a runner. All the same always remember to get a proper receipt with an address and phone number where you can contact them later if necessary.

● Antique fairs. THESE ARE AT THE TOP END OF THE SCALE. Many of them might look grand because often the venues are grand (such as the Grosvenor House Hotel in Mayfair where the top 100 *crème de la crème* dealers set out their exquisite wares) but don't be put off. To use our hunt for a little walnut spoon-backed chair as an example again: if you go to a big antiques fair

there will be a large collection of dealers displaying their wares to the best of their advantage in an open market-place environment. It might be rather swish, with stands and curtains, but it is still a market-place and they are there to sell. You are there to look and possibly buy in your own time, when you are ready.

Not everything for sale is expensive. Goods on sale at places like Grosvenor House are so appealing that at the end of the first day (when some say in excess of £100 million changes hands) stocks have to be replenished.

All kinds come on the stands. Some of them are incredibly wealthy, people who can count their fortune in billions. But I want to say to all of you who make more modest livings that even though I am showing you a lot of glamorous, expensive items in this book, I and all the other hard-working dealers also sell much more modest pieces. I'm only too happy to spend time with anybody from any walk of life in any price range. Prices have risen considerably, but I still think you can find very nice small pieces of furniture or decorative items from about £500 and go from there. It is possible to find a nice single 19th-century carved chair within that price range, for instance, or a lovely mirror that will grace your home; you won't always get an oil but you can get a magnificent signed watercolour. The other day I bought a delightful little Italian picture frame in perfect condition, inlaid with shells, that will sell for about £400. There are lots of nice things you can buy even at the most rarefied shows. The range of objects might surprise you.

What you can depend on at these fairs is quality. At fairs of this standard because you will get a properly headed bill of sale with a full description of what you have bought so you can always contact the dealer at his shop or home base and get your money back.

Speaking for myself, in the months leading up to a big fair I am digging very deep, searching all over the country for things of quality, desirable items that I believe to be valuable and that customers will want. I'm always looking for something that's just a little different or exotic because there will be 400 competitors at the fair.

Knowing what my customers want comes from years of experience in the trade, of selling antiques to the public and having a very good eye. I'm not just buying something commercial (that is, something that is readily saleable); I'm buying what I believe in. I have the confidence to do this from years of buying and selling items. I have found that if I buy what I believe in and really like, I can talk to potential customers with genuine honesty and passion. It makes life easier for me, because when I like something I'm excited about it, and I can transfer that excitement to my clients because it's from the heart. I have a feeling that people 'suss' you out very quickly when you talk in half-muted tones about something that you don't have a genuine regard for. If you don't like a piece, why should they?

From years of being reliable I have built up a solid base of clients who trust me. I'm telling you this because when you go to a reputable fair you will learn by looking at the very best, genuine articles and a novice can distil years of the joint experience of dozens of dealers if he or she looks learns, listens and asks the right questions – you will almost always buy a piece that is what it is supposed to be.

● **Ask questions.** IF YOU SEE SOMETHING YOU LIKE, ask as many questions as you like, just as you did when you were getting your eye in. Don't be shy. There's nothing like a bit of flattery. People, including me, like to be told that the pieces they are exhibiting are lovely. If you go on to someone's stand and say, 'Can I have a look at your rubbish?' you'll have an appropriate reaction. At one show, a really obnoxious bumptious type walked on to a neighbouring stand run by a friend of mine. With his neighing haw-haw voice, it was, 'What is this laddy? What is that, hmm?'

My chum said, 'Oh, that's a Regency curtain pole.'

'Hmm' said Mr Bumptious. 'Tell me about it, laddy – go on laddy, what is it?'

'Well, sir, it's wonderfully carved, it has these original brass bits – '

'Any provenance, hmm? Any provenance, laddy?'

Losing patience my chum said, 'As matter of fact, sir, there is a provenance. I bought it off the back of a K-reg Volvo in a car park on the M6.' Mr Bumptious slunk off and wasn't seen in that part of the fair again.

So go about with a little bit of cunning, use a little bit of tact and charm, and you'll find the dealers eating out of your hand.

At the same time, tell the dealer frankly that you will be looking at several other alternatives. Don't say it in such a way that it comes out like a threat, just make it honest. 'I'm going to look at several spoon-backed chairs. Within the next twenty-four hours I'm going to make my mind up and buy one.' In other words someone is going to get your hard-earned money – and it's a question of who. If the dealer wants your money he's going to work for it by telling you all you want to know about that chair and also by offering to knock a bit off. Tell him you will want a proper receipt and a guarantee. If a dealer is snooty and refuses to do any of these things, be strict with yourself and walk away. You've come to a large open-air market with hundreds of other stands, such as the famous Newark sale, or to a town where there are plenty of other antiques shops stuffed with a large variety of goods from which you will be able to make an informed choice. There are plenty of competitors out there who will be very happy to sell to you.

A lot of people are nervous about following this advice. They are scared of being a nuisance, or of looking silly. But there is an easy way of going about it. Politeness is a great winding sheet. 'Would you do this – could you show me that, could you turn it upside down? I don't know what I'm looking for yet, but I'm hoping you'll show me what you have. I want to have a really good look at this chair.' If you charm the dealer he is more than likely to let you have a jolly good look, and point out a few faults if there are any and offer you advice. Genuine dealers will go out of their way not to rook you but to help you – after all, they want your custom and they hope you might come back year after year.

Some of my best customers have wandered on to my stand looking as if they didn't have a penny to their name. A few years ago at Olympia an old man with tanned, wrinkled skin came toddling by in a bright blue jacket with brass buttons and a little white cap with braid on it. I don't know why, but I nodded and said, 'Good morning, Captain.' I didn't know that he actually owned a yacht, as well as a fleet of tankers. He nodded back and stepped on to my stand. He looked a little weary, so I invited him to sit, which he did, while I got on with chatting to another client. The 'Captain' turned out to be a Greek shipping tycoon, who brought some beautiful pieces from me that day, perhaps because I didn't pressure him. When he had chosen several pieces and departed, I had to run after him with the invoice. 'Excuse me, who are you?' I asked. 'How will you pay?' His secretary looked astonished, as if to say you must be the only person here today who doesn't know John Latsis, billionaire! He bought many more pieces from me over the years.

I was at a fair once in Birmingham when a lady I can only describe as being a Margaret Rutherford character came on to the stand – in fact I thought it *was* Margaret Rutherford. She was quite heavy in posture with the Rutherford tweeds, large pull-down squashy hat, heavy lisle-type stockings wrinkled and buckled as though she was wearing two or three pairs, and a plastic shopping bag. She was quite eccentric; you almost could see her in the *VIPs* with Elizabeth Taylor and Richard Burton in the scene at the airport where someone says to the old bat, 'I can't find you on the check-in list' and suddenly a supervisor comes up and says, 'Good afternoon, your Grace – she's in first class.'

Anyway, on the stand were a very fine quartetto of delicate Sheraton tables, dated about 1780, in a nest from which they can all slide out. 'Miss Rutherford' stomped up to these tables and began to drag them out quite roughly. I could see their long fragile legs about to break so I said, 'Excuse me, madam, may I help you?' I slid them out gently and let her have a good look. In her deep voice she asked how much they were. £5,700, I informed her. She rumbled, 'Mmm, hmm, hmm,' then left. She came back four or five times. Each time, I nodded at her, 'Nice to see you, madam.' Each time, she dragged at the tables – in fact, she was doing exactly what I have told you to do: inspect, inspect, inspect, go away and come back again; but I would hope you would treat the items with more care. 'Let me assist you,' I would say, coming forward and gently taking the tables from her clumsy hands. In my mind I was thinking, 'She's going to smash these tables, she's not going to buy them and soon they'll be matchwood.' But nevertheless I persevered and was polite because that's what you're there for and really, she wasn't a bad old sort.

I almost reeled into the tables with shock when on the final visit she said. 'Well, I suppose you'll take £5,500 for them?' Recovering quickly, I said 'I would indeed.' She signed a cheque and after she left someone came across to me and said. 'Do you know who that is?' I had to confess that I did not. She was one of the richest women in Warwickshire. Every year she'd come to this fair and buy something of really superior quality. That year, I was the lucky lad who was chosen. If I had been impatient with her and told her to clear off, to leave my tables alone before she broke them, I would not have been chosen. Which just goes to show.

● Don't be pressurized. THIS IS A GOLDEN RULE IN ANY BUYING SITUATION. Many people prefer to wander around a fair or market because they are somewhat intimidated when they go to a shop and have to ring a bell. At a fair there's no door bell and no pressure from sales staff. If you are someone with less confidence, remember that you can walk from stand to stand without obligation and if anyone puts any pressure on you before you are ready, you can simply walk off. A good dealer won't pressure you. If a dealer does try to pressure you, whatever happens, don't be pushed into making a decision on the spot – remember Auntie Wainwright. Go away, look for other similar pieces, compare them, then come back. If you miss it, you miss it; there'll always be another piece, possibly a nicer one – that's the thrill of the antiques' hunt.

At a fair there is a lively atmosphere with healthy competition – competition that can work for you as well as against you. Anything up to 30,000 people attend the bigger fairs, so if you spot something that appeals to you don't wait too long to make an offer. On the other hand, depending on the size and the grandeur of the fair, the dealers have often paid a great deal of money to be there for that day or that week, from the rent of their stand to such overheads as accommodation, transport and insurance, and they are anxious to sell.

● Ask for the very best price. SUPPOSE YOU HAVE SEEN SOMETHING on a particular stand that appeals to your eye. You have asked all the right questions and the dealer has said he will give you a detailed receipt. If that piece is still there when you go back, you can say, 'I have walked past your stand a couple of times and last time I was here, you very kindly answered all my questions. I see that the piece I am interested in is still here. But I have to tell you that I've also seen two or three similar pieces elsewhere at this fair. I'm a little embarrassed to say this, but although I like this one the best, it is a little more than I budgeted for. What is your very best price?'

That phrase, *your very best price*, is a term that dealers themselves frequently use and it means the lowest price at which a piece can be sold. Often, it never occurs to people that they can negotiate a price in this way.

On another occasion at Olympia an American and his wife walked onto my stand on the opening day with their interior decorator in tow. They unrolled the blueprints of the new mansion they were building in Beverly Hills and inspected my matching pair of Cantonese Chinese export Regency period (1830s) coffers below. They were looking for two free-standing coffers decorated on all sides, which mine were, to use as tables next to a bed that was to be set in the middle of the room. They drove a very hard bargain,

*C*hinese long coffers. $30 million for the house and they still knocked me down!

managing to get me down from the asking price of £7,000 to £6,000, all the while telling me about the $30 million they were lavishing on their nouveau palace. They wanted those two coffers and wouldn't leave until they had pared me down to the bone with a 'Take it or leave it buddy.' I was conscious of the rent of my stand and dinner to buy that evening, so I took it. I wish I could have said, 'I'm leaving it, buddy.'

People ask me if it is better to go to a fair on the first or the last day, I tell them, it all depends, which might not be a very helpful answer, but it really does depend. If you miss the first day you might miss some good things. Also on the first day a dealer is very much aware of his high overheads; perhaps he is worried that he won't break even. So, even on the first day he is looking to cover his costs. If you came to me on the last part of the fair whether we'd had a successful fair or not, like a lot of dealers at that stage we would probably be amenable to striking a bargain with you rather than taking the goods back home. I have often sold everything except for one or two pieces – a good fair – but I am still happy to negotiate.

My experience has shown me that more than half of the people who go to these fairs are there looking for a specific item, yet, suddenly they fall for something completely different – such as a lovely brass standard lamp when before they would never in their wildest dreams have thought of owning one. For these people, an antiques fair is like an Aladdin's cave – certainly it is more like a bazaar than the hushed environment of an antiques shop. And when this happens all of a sudden, they turn into enthusiastic bargain hunters.

I know I told you earlier to decide what you want and stick to it, but when you're feeling more confident, I think that, provided you are not too rash, it is actually not a bad thing to have an open mind if you are in a safe environment like a shop or a fair. (An auction, where auction fever can get hold of you, is another matter altogether – see page 88.)

THE CHINA AFFAIR

SOME YEARS AGO I bought at the Irish antiques fair in Dublin a very rare, life-size figure of a female mandarin dated 1790, The figure came originally from an East India trading family who owned a large Irish country house. I had never seen anything like it; and in fact, since then I have learned of only one other figure, a male mandarin, possibly its pair, in the Peabody Museum in Massachusetts I think. I believe that they were made to show the Western world what Orientals looked like. My female figure was quite exquisite, with a serene face that had a most life-like expression. Like the Mona Lisa, her eyes seemed to follow you. Under her traditional original silk robes, her body was fairly crude, stuffed with a mixture of clay and straw, but the parts that you could see – the head, the arms and the feet (which were replicas of the tiny bound feet of Chinese women) – were made of glazed earthenware; and the head nodded. At the Olympia fair she attracted a great deal of attention and I sold her at the preview for £19,000, but, as was customary, retained her for the opening day, placing her carefully to one side on my stand.

I WASN'T AWARE that Princess Margaret had arrived with her entourage until one of the fair organizers deftly reached round behind me and removed the drink I was holding – even though the princess herself had a glass of gin and a cigarette in a long holder. I was introduced, and she asked several

questions about the various pieces I had on display. My confidence was growing and, thinking it would intrigue her, since I was aware that she had recently made a state visit to China, I said,

'Oh, ma'am, may I point out to you this extraordinary figure which I sold at the preview?'

THE PRINCESS looked at it carefully. It was of course quite still, so I was electrified when Her Royal Highness turned to me and asked, 'Does it nod its head?'

I WAS AMAZED, thinking to myself, 'Blimey, she's knowledgeable!' . Perhaps she had seen a similar figure in the Summer Palace in Peking and would be able to give me a few tips about its history. I said, 'It does indeed, ma'am. Have you seen one of these before?'

SHE SAID, 'Yes, I've seen one in china.' (She pronounced it 'chi-nar'.)

MY MIND was racing as I said, 'Well, ma'am, *this* came from China in the late 18th century.'

SHE LOOKED at me as if she was a bit puzzled and said, 'No, I've seen them in china.'

WHEN SHE REPEATED that, I thought she hadn't heard me clearly, so I moved very close to her and leaned down to say quite distinctly in her ear, 'As I said, ma'am, *this* came from China in the late 18th century.'

SHE LOOKED quite frustrated and brought up her hand as if in emphasis and said loudly, 'No, I've seen them in china!'

SUDDENLY it hit me: the upper crust don't say 'porcelain', they say 'china'. Princess Margaret was referring to the face and arms of the figure, which were indeed made of earthenware, which can look like china, as she would call it. She probably had seen several similar figures, but most likely far smaller ones, in the Queen's extensive doll collection, for example.

DURING this exchange, the Princess had been smoking her cigarette in its elegant holder and now looked around for an ashtray, which I didn't have on my stand. I was taken aback when an equerry hurried forward, grovelled low and held out his cupped hand. I was mesmerized, surely she wasn't about to stub her cigarette out on his palm? No – HRH flicked her ash into it, smiled graciously at me and moved on.

I COULD IMAGINE her at some dinner party that night saying, 'I met that peculiar David Dickinson at Olympia, and he would not stop repeating himself!'

The Antiques Buyer

4

Buying at Auction

When I first started out, dealers dominated auction sales, both as bidders and as sellers: often 95 per cent of any auction consisted of the trade with just five per cent of the public, who felt like outsiders, as indeed they were. I have to say it: dealers wanted to preserve the mystique, they wanted the public to buy their goods in their expensive shops. They didn't want the auction bartering to be seen in case (perish the thought!) customers in their shops started to haggle.

Television shows such as the Antiques Roadshow, and even my own television series, have changed all that. Since the 1980s auction sales of every type have become far more accessible to the public, to the extent that the proportion of dealers to ordinary people at auctions is now often reversed when collectables are being sold.

Even so, too many people going to an auction is a terrifying prospect; many people still feel as if they are entering hallowed ground where the rituals and special language established by the high priest and the initiated (the auctioneer and the dealers) will baffle and confuse them. If you feel like this, the answer is join them. Learn the language (it's all here in this book) and understand what they're on about. That way you will feel comfortable in that environment and you will no longer be an outsider.

Antiques auctions of all types are a rich source of goods, but always a minefield to the uninitiated. That doesn't mean that *you* can't take part and go to an auction or enjoy the thrill of bidding and eventually buying and taking home your desired object. You can, but don't be naïve. Learn to walk first of all before you run. And remember, there are guys like me around bidding against you, professionals who've had twenty, thirty years experience, so it's not as easy as all that.

These days auction houses are geared to help the first-time buyer and,

*S*old for £5 million to the gentleman who's just scratched his nose in the fifth row! Don't worry, it doesn't happen in real life. It is very difficult to have a bid accepted by mistake. Remember, you are in control.

despite what people say about scratching your nose and ending up with a Picasso, you are always in control: you and you alone decide whether to make that all-important bid or not. There is no doubt that auctions are conducted at such a rattling pace that panic can set in, and I must warn you that your first experience at an auction is nearly always nerve-racking. Not only is the first time you take a deep breath and raise your catalogue to catch the auctioneer's eye a bit like making your first speech in public, but as the tension of listening to the other bids climb up and up you can get clammy hands and feel sick. But if you have done your homework, know the ground rules and keep outwardly calm, all will go well.

What is an auction?

Essentially, there are five kinds of auction where you can buy antiques:

● *Quality auctions*, usually at the major auction houses where nothing but the best antiques – from furniture to paintings – are ever offered.

● *General sales*, where anything and everything from old to new – from that Greek urn to the kitchen sink – is up for sale.

● *Country house sales*, where the contents of that house are exclusively for sale *in situ*.

● *Specialists and collectors' sales*, where you can go to bid for anything from garden and architectural pieces, stamps, carpets and rugs to ceramics or jewellery.

● *Private homes and small business sales*, which are not as grand as country houses, and can include the contents of any kind of residence – from farms or seaside bungalows to family hotels that have gone broke.

There are other kinds of auction sales where antiques hunting is possible, such as bankrupt stock sales, the ones conducted by the police consisting of unclaimed stolen goods, or unclaimed lost property sales held by the railway or bus companies, but in these places antiques will be thin on the ground so generally, you can disregard them if you are in search of a particular item. However, they are interesting to go to and there is always the very remote possibility that you might stumble across some unrecognized treasure. At least you'll have one advantage: it is most unlikely that there will be much competition from dealers in such sales.

Where to find them

Trade newspapers and magazines have completely changed the face of the antiques business. In the old days a local dealer might have been the kingpin of his district. He knew what was going on and, if anything special turned up in that area like the disposal of a house's contents, he would have it, or the cream of it, often sending the best items down to London to the big auction houses and making a handsome profit. Nowadays, with all trade newspapers and magazines advertising everything that's available, it's very much a free-for-all. Aware of what is coming up in the saleroom, people travel the country. Often now in a saleroom there'll be three or four phone calls, one from Hong Kong, two from America and one from France. The Internet has enabled many dealers to cast an even wider web.

It is worth pointing out here that many provincial auctioneers 'hold over' certain goods instead of putting them in a general sale. These are usually finer quality antiques, which they will 'save up' to lump together in one of the finer quality sales they hold perhaps two or three times a year to give their establishment some kudos and a bit of glamour.

For the seller the benefits are that these finer-quality sales are more widely advertised, and so more dealers will attend and the competition may be fiercer. The disadvantages are that your goods might sit around unsold for a considerable time, waiting for the sale. Sometimes, items that have been identified as being of particular interest and value might be whisked off to one of the provincial saleroom's big London branches. Again, this can be advantageous to the seller in that it will be properly identified and advertised.

For a buyer, there are pros and cons to this system. At a little local sale, where prices can be low, you can often get a good bargain; but prices can also be high if not much is for sale, when dealers might bid very strongly against each other out of pure boredom and a sense of competition. Equally, I have found that London prices can sometimes be surprisingly low because so much high-quality material is on offer. At the end of the day it really can be pot luck which way the market goes.

The first league salerooms are the big London ones. These also have smaller salerooms in major centres up and down the country. The big auction houses have many general antiques sales where an eclectic selection of quality goods are sold; they also pride themselves on their numerous specialist sales where one type of goods come up for sale perhaps once a year. The advantages of these specialist sales for a collector is that objects in your field are pulled together under one roof from all over the country, and perhaps even the world. Equally, the advantage for a seller is that there you will find the cream of collectors' items. The first-league salerooms are: Bonham's, Christie's, Sotheby's and Phillips.

A list of the second-league salerooms around the country, as well as the third and fourth league, and also a very useful list of specialist dealers, can be found in numerous trade publications such as *The Antique Gazette*.

I never seem to lose my passion for this business or get jaded. I go to a sale and the old adrenaline and excitement surges through me again. Sometimes I can barely control the excitement. Many times I have had to take a deep breath to calm myself down. In my head I can hear myself saying, 'I love it, I

BUYING AT AUCTION
– ON LINE

AN OLD TRADITIONALIST like me finds computers and the Internet a complete mystery. But let's face it, there is no doubt it is the future of retailing. At the time of writing even the venerable house of Sotheby's is now holding auctions on the Internet! But be warned: auctions on the Internet can be great fun but the opportunities for fraud are huge and you should be very careful.

So how do they work?

THE PRINCIPLE is the same on all auction web sites. You register, you are given a secure access code, which only you know, and away you go. Each item is auctioned from a particular time and date and proceeds for a set amount of time. If you have any questions not answered in the descriptions, you e-mail the seller before committing to a bid. There may or may not be a reserve and there may be increments which you have to bid in. If your bid is exceeded most sites have a mechanism whereby the computer automatically e-mails you of the new bid and asks if you want to continue. At the end of the auction, the venue will exchange e-mail addresses of the seller and highest bidder. The seller and buyer then contact each other to get the appropriate address information in order to exchange the payment and merchandise.

ONLINE AUCTIONS can be a fun way to shop, but remember that it is important to practice safe buying and selling when you are online. Just like real flesh and blood auctions 'virtual' actions have their do's and don'ts. Use caution and common sense. The most common major problems are with merchandise never delivered; item misrepresented; goods damaged in shipment or defective. Ask yourself: is what the seller promises realistic? Is this the best way to buy this item? What is the most I am willing to bid for it? Reputable auction houses such as Sotheby's have their reputations to consider and they auction goods with all the guarantees they would give in a flesh and blood auction.

The following tips, should help:

FIRST THERE'S the obvious one: you cannot actually handle and see for yourself what you are buying. Sure, on some web sites you can zoom in and move around the object, but like looking in a catalogue you cannot see the blemishes, bumps and bashes.

UNDERSTAND how the auction works. Go through the instructions on the website carefully. Use the e-mail enquiry service if you have any questions.

MANY ON-LINE auctions simply list items that people want to sell. They don't verify if the merchandise actually exists or is described accurately. Remember that auction web sites are merely 'venues' therefore, if you feel at all unsure about a transaction, ask the seller to put the item and payment with a third party who can verify the item is what it is supposed to be and that the money is paid. Some venues are able to offer such an 'escrow service'.

CHECK OUT the seller. If the seller is based in the United States contact the local consumer protection agency in the appropriate state. Look at the auction site's feedback section for comments about the seller. Look out for bogus ones from the seller themselves.

BE ESPECIALLY careful if the seller is a private individual. It's very difficult to track down individuals who abscond. Get a physical address and other identifying information from the seller. Don't do business with sellers who won't provide that information.

SINCE YOU can't examine the item or have it appraised until after the sale, you can't assume that claims made about it are valid. Insist on getting a written statement describing the item and its value before you pay.

IF YOU WIN the auction the buyer should ask about delivery, returns, warranties and service. Get a definite delivery time and insist that the shipment be insured. Ask about the return policy. If you're buying electronic goods or appliances, find out if there is a warranty and how to get service. Sellers usually include their payment and delivery terms in the description of the product.

PAY THE safest way. Requesting cash is a clear sign of fraud. If possible, pay by credit card because you can dispute the charges if the goods are misrepresented or never arrive. Or use an escrow agent, who acts as a go-between to receive the merchandise and forward your payment to the seller. Another option is cash on delivery (COD). Pay by check made out to the seller, so you can stop payment if necessary.

LOOK ON the World Wide Web for the Internet Fraud Watch site (www.fraud.org/ifw.htm). This will give you other tips about buying safely over the net.

HERE ARE a couple of good sites to visit. I would not presume to recommend them but you may find them interesting.
www.ebay.com
www.amazon.com

The Antiques Buyer

love it and I've got to have it!' This almost drooling enthusiasm isn't always good commercial sense, but I feel that if I can be enthusiastic about something, there must be something wonderful about it, and if I can infuse my clients with that passion, I will have given them something special too, a genuine love for the pieces they buy.

I've always been a little bit daring in that sense in business. I will go out and if I've got an allocation of money I will spend it all. Some people are a little more careful; they will keep some back for a rainy day. Before a sale has even begun they think, 'If I don't sell anything on again I'll be in a pickle, and I'm sure it infiltrates their attitude. I've always believed that you must get out there and pitch. Being on a knife-edge is part of the glamour and excitement of the game. Not everybody can take it – it can lead to depression and I've seen it crack people up – but I thrive on it. I also find that I don't make as many mistakes when it's costing me money. If I do make mistakes it's amazing how quickly I start to compensate for them and spend more time studying and inspecting because I know that not doing so enough can be costly for me.

The old dealers know all this, in fact, I'm just passing on to you what they passed on to me. 'You've got to back your own judgement,' they told me time and time again when I was starting out. There will be a time when you get a certain amount of confidence, and you will look at the points you've been told to look for, but there will also be a time when you're less confident and you've got to stand on your two feet for better or for worse. Don't be put off if you make a mistake; if you do, you've got to go back in there. There is no substitute for perseverance and you will build your confidence as you become more experienced.

And before I take you step by step through a typical auction (see page 89), let me give you the following very specific and helpful rules, which have stood me in good stead over the years.

Ten Golden Rules

1 Go to the preview

To decide what you want to buy, do your leg work. Find out where an auction is being held where you can find what it is you are interested in by looking in the trade press, appropriate glossy magazines or in local newspapers. Then go to the viewing (see page 89). This will give you plenty of time to look, examine and ask questions. There is no sense in bidding for something that you have not thoroughly inspected. Even if you are a beginner, this inspection will tell you far more than you realized you knew. Have a cup of coffee, go back and have another look. Then sleep on it.

2 *Get a condition report*

This is invaluable if you are a beginner. You can ask the auctioneer to give you one (see page 89). For a substantial piece, you can ask a dealer you know and pay him.

3 *On the day of the sale, get there in good time and register*

Many people arrive late and miss the boat. Even if the item you are bidding for is to be auctioned late in the sale, you will still gain a lot from familiarizing yourself with the saleroom environment and watching the prices. You must register because when you do you will be given a paddle or a card with a number on it to hold up so that the auctioneer can keep track of who is bidding for what.

4 *Know what you want and bid only for the pieces that you have inspected*

This sounds like unnecessary advice, but you'd be surprised how many people change their mind at the last moment and start to bid for something they haven't inspected. Or, if they have lost the piece they were after, they are determined to go home with something for their pains but frequently end up with any old rubbish.

Even when I know what I want at an auction, I will often inspect several other likely pieces that I am undecided about. If the bidding for any of those pieces is sluggish I will sometimes bid for it, but not unless I have thoroughly inspected it first. I did have a disaster once which taught me a lesson I've never forgotten (see page 102). If you don't inspect the piece before bidding, don't be surprised if you end up with rubbish. It is far better to walk away than buy a turkey – there will always be other sales and other antiques to buy.

5 *Have a budget and stick to it*

Again, in the frenzy of the moment you might be determined to buy something at any cost. The trouble is that it might cost you dear, far more than you can afford or the piece is worth. Sometimes people are very circumspect and buy their piece within their budget, but then, fired with success, they go auction crazy and bid for the next six lots. Don't.

6 *Don't lose what you want for a bid*

This is the converse of rule five, but there are times when rule five doesn't apply – when acquiring an item means more than the price. If a piece is special to you, go for it. That one last bid might win the day. But don't go crazy. Use your instinct, judge when to continue that last half-inch and when to stop. Even having said that, I would say that sometimes, if you really fall in love with something, you should buy it no matter what the cost. It might end up costing more than you can afford, but the price won't be unrealistic in the market-place because it is a truism that the market value will be just one bid more than the next bidder. At times like that you have to let your heart rule your head or else you will always regret it.

7 *Go for quality*

I've said it before and I'll say it again. Quality counts. It is the reason you are buying antiques.

8 *Let the auctioneer know that you are bidding*

It used to be said that people wore false moustaches at auctions and twitched an eyebrow to indicate a bid, but unless you are bidding for a Renoir worth millions and feel the need to fool the opposition, such games are unnecessary. Let the auctioneer see that you are bidding by raising your catalogue or paddle; if you don't he might miss your obscure signal. And when you have finished bidding, tell him 'No' with a firm shake of your head.

9 *Don't get auction fever*

I've seen this so many times. It's like a feeding frenzy at the zoo or the Klondike gold rush. The most rational people can suddenly bid for everything at any price. Reality only hits home when they see how much they have spent and realize they have to arrange the transport home of half the contents of the auction room. Don't do it.

10 *Remember the hidden costs*

The buyer's commission or premium varies from one saleroom to another. Generally it's 15 per cent. It should be in the catalogue. If it's not, find out what it is when you register and mentally add it on to your bid. VAT is standard – currently 17½ per cent on the commission only, not on the full bid price. Transport can also prove expensive. Take it all into account – it can add up to an extra £18 on every £100 under the hammer.

You also need to check removal time. Normally, if you leave your goods hanging around the auction room for more than 24 hours you will be charged storage.

Taking the plunge

If you feel intimidated by auctions, first attend an auction without even thinking of buying. Inspect at the preview, watch the sale go through, watch the prices. Get the feel of it. When you feel ready, if you hear of a sale and see something in the catalogue you like, and the estimates are within a price range to suit your pocket, it would be fine to dip your toes into the water and plan on making that first crucial bid.

I use the word 'plan' because that is exactly what you should do. Say you want to buy a table, as I once did many years ago when I was furnishing my first home. The first thing to do is go to the preview and inspect that table thoroughly. Put your hands on it and feel the wood. Is that a century of hand waxing, or is that modern varnish? Get a sense of the weight; solid mahogany and oak are heavy. What about the way the table stands – does it wobble, and are the legs uneven or loose? Look underneath, a place that restorers and fakers often neglect: is it held together with new brackets or odd blocks of wood, or is there fresh stain? Good common sense will tell you if you can say to yourself, 'Well that looks pretty good value for money to me. They're saying £400–£600 – and remember, add 18 per cent. I can afford that. It seems like a very nice piece of furniture for that price range.'

At this stage there are a number of things you need to know about auction sales – and the way they work and the options available to you.

Condition report

You're not an antiques expert, but you've got plenty of grey matter up there, and it's a matter of just applying it. If you lack experience and knowledge and you are thinking of bidding for a very expensive piece, there is a very easy way of safeguard yourself: call a representative of the saleroom, either the saleroom manager or, with the bigger salerooms, the head of department, and ask for a condition report. This is perfectly normal and they won't throw up their hands in horror at being asked. A condition report is a written or verbal statement about the piece you are interested in. In simple language it will describe it, say what it is, give the date or approximate date of manufacture, tell you any faults and give a value based on the expert's experience and the market-place.

Representation

You might consider visiting a local antiques dealer to represent you in the saleroom. If you do agree a fee or a commission, he will go to the preview and advise you on what to bid for. In this way you can utilize his experience in exactly the same way as you would get the AA to vet a car you want to buy, or a surveyor to inspect a house before you take out a mortgage. People are used to doing such things as a matter of course, yet it never occurs to them to do the same for a table and a set of chairs that might cost £2,000 or £3,000.

For those with little time, a good dealer can save a client a lot of time and trouble. Of course everyone is in the business to make money – it would be foolish to deny it – but because of his greater expertise a dealer can actually save you money.

You can also ask someone from the auction house to represent you at the sale. On the day of the sale you will probably notice that not all bids are from the floor. In a grand sale, especially if an important picture or *objet d'art* is being auctioned, you might notice a battery of saleroom assistants lined up on telephones. They will be taking telephone bids from absentee buyers or clients who are on the other end of the telephone – perhaps people from overseas, who could not attend in person, people who do not wish their identity to be known by their rivals. Another way of making an absentee bid, one known as a *commission bid*, is to pre-arrange your bid with the auctioneer. Suppose, for example, that a piece has been estimated at £4,000–£5,000. You might be prepared to go up to £8,000. The final bid from the floor or the telephone is £7,500. The auctioneer will then bring your bid into play and you win the day. Of course, if someone else comes in at £8,500 you are gazumped and they win.

But these kind of deals are for the high-flyers. My advice to you would be to always attend in person or you will never get the feel of this business; and even with all my experience I personally would be very reluctant to be an absentee bidder. In my opinion there is nothing so satisfying as a hands-on approach when you're dealing with antiques.

The reserve price

This is the lowest price that the seller will accept. The auctioneer sets it, using his experience in conjunction with the seller. Some auctioneers are renowned for valuing low, the advantage being that it attracts a lot more people, especially in the trade. If I see that a local auctioneer has put a pair of 19th-century library globes at £4,000–£6.000, and I know on a bad day they're worth £12,000, I will go rushing along to the auction, along with all the other dealers. Ten to one, at the end of the day the globes will make £16,000, perhaps because a little competition gets going in that room full of dealers. But this approach can be very misleading to a private person, who is led to believe that the guide of £4,000–£6,000 is where they should be pitching their bids.

Some sellers will argue with the auctioneer. They think that if they put down a very high reserve it will automatically lead to the auctioneer setting a higher estimate. The auctioneer might say, 'Madam, this ashtray you've brought along is very nice and I think it should fetch £400–£600.' Mrs Smythe-Jones replies, 'Well, I was hoping to get a bit more than that, Mr Robinson,' to which the auctioneer might say, 'Well, we could try £600–£800, with a reserve of £600 if you give me a little flexibility.' But normally, the auctioneer will advise the seller to keep it to the lower estimate because the auction house gets commission only if it sells the goods. Auctioneers also like to surprise the client by saying, 'By the way, that ashtray that we said £400–£600, there was a great demand for it and it made £1,200.' To which, if the script is written as he hopes, Mrs Smythe-Jones will reply, 'I'm very pleased, Mr Robinson. I'll bring along some more of my very nice things for you to sell in your saleroom.'

The sale price

If I go into a saleroom and I see a table estimated at £400–£600 my experience of hundreds of similar tables tells me whether that's a reasonable estimate or not. Sometimes I may look at that table and recognize that there is something special about it, and it's often an intangible thing. I will say to myself, 'What a beauty! That's the nicest example I have ever seen.'

When the bidding passes £600 and gets up to £1,500, then £2,200 then £2,800 I don't blink and keep going. My experience has kicked in and is telling me to keep bidding because I know that's the best example I've seen in twenty-odd years. I may never see another one with that same quality, so I'll give a strong price to buy it. This is where the *pocket and the heart* come in.

If you are a private individual who has been guided by the £400–£600 price range, you're comfortable within that framework, but once the bidding starts spiralling way beyond that you become confused. You think, 'What's going on?' This is why the professional has a great advantage: his experience and knowledge kicks in to tell him to keep bidding long after the novice has dropped out. This is not always the case. Sometimes a private buyer with a lot of money gets caught up in the chase and senses the excitement. He says to himself, 'I want that. If they can bid, so can I. If it's worth £2,200 to a dealer, who must sell at a profit, it's worth that to me.' Entrepreneurial instincts take over and the private buyer sticks in there. The auction environment can be a very exciting and stimulating one and many people who would never dream of throwing their money away in a casino get into auction frenzy. Believe me, I've seen it happen. I have even seen husband and wife bid against each other unaware that the other is bidding. I am painting an exceptional scenario here, but it is one that you might encounter. I do not recommend that you join the chase. Remember rule five: *have a budget and stick to it.*

Competition

For no apparent reason, some sales attract an awful lot of attention from dealers and they swarm to the sale from all over the country like bees to a honey pot. Sometimes 20 to 30 dealers gathering at an auction is fine if there are plenty of quality goods available to be shared out. But if quality is thin on the ground they start to battle it out for the most ordinary pieces and prices can spiral out of all proportion to the value. For the innocent amateur what happens can be quite baffling. Just bear in mind that sometimes these things do happen and, if you are a beginner at your very first auction, stick to my rules and don't let such a situation put you off.

A typical situation is when I go to what seems to be a very inexpensive saleroom in the middle of a cattleyard somewhere, drawn there by information from my runner who has spotted a 'sleeper'. It's a late Regency cabinet that has been lying in an attic for a century and is so encrusted with dirt that you don't know what it is; but the original pristine piece is underneath in all its glory, just waiting to be rediscovered with a little judicious restoration. But other runners who work for other dealers have also spotted that cabinet. On my arrival to preview I think, 'That little beauty is coming home with me – these guys here with straw in their hair certainly won't be recognizing this.' But during the time while I wait around for the sale to start, other dealers start popping up from behind chiffoniers and I realize there's going to be a terrible massacre.

If you've got up at the crack of dawn, driven for three hours, viewed the material, stayed another three hours until the sale commences and then have another three hours' drive home after your lot has been dispensed with, it can make for a lot more determination. The same thing applies to your competitors. 'Aw my Gawd, there's so and so! I've come all this way down here to buy this cabinet and I'm not going to leave without it.'

Sometimes, good sense and all the lessons I've been teaching you kick in and I walk away. We've all had our moments of madness though, so don't feel too upset if you get a touch of auction fever from time to time.

Runners

Someone you might see at an auction sale is a runner. Runners were a good system in the past when there were no trade newspapers or magazines. You still find them today: people who make a living by going round all sorts of outlets for antiques, spotting goods and calling the appropriate dealers. They live by getting commission, the amount of which varies, depending on how much the dealer makes; it may not be a percentage on the value of the item, but could still be a few hundred pounds, especially if they have directed the dealer to a very good or interesting piece.

How much is it worth?

If you're thinking of selling something at auction, you'll want to know, before you decide, what the piece is likely to fetch. You can buy books filled with photographs of items of every category of antiques, decorative items and memorabilia from salerooms the length and breadth of the

British Isles, together with the price they fetched on the day of sale. I'm not sure what this information tells you, because something can bring a very good price and if that price is then inserted in the book you presume that that is the going price for an 18th-century walnut bureau bookcase, or whatever, but it may not be the case. The one in the book could be a real corker that is worth, say, £36,000. You think, 'Ah, that's the price.' But it's not true for a very poor one in terrible condition that goes for £4,000–£5,000. Or the one in the book wasn't a corker – it just made a high price because it was a good day.

Using price guides can work against you. Say you have a prized 18th-century walnut bureau bookcase at home that you inherited from your great-aunt. You look in one of these price-guide books, and your eyes light up. You hadn't intended to sell, but now, with a potential £36,000 staring you in the face, you decide that you will, so that you can buy that cottage in France or pay for your daughter's school fees. Then, when the auctioneer advises you it will not get much above £6,000 and at the auction it reaches only £4,000, who do you blame, the auctioneer or the book? Certainly you might feel you're being cheated in some way, but in fact it is virtually impossible to say how much something is worth just by comparing it with a photograph in a book of something you don't know the condition of.

If I were to take three identical bookcases such as the lovely little French one that I have in my sitting room at home and place them in three different auctions in this country, they would bring three totally different prices that would not only be based on their present condition, but would also depend on the competition at the saleroom on that particular day.

You can learn a lot from price-guide books about size, shape, materials and style. Use them as a rough guide to price by all means, but don't depend on them. Using them is not as good as getting out there yourself, asking questions, seeking advice and learning by your own experience.

Buyer beware

In a saleroom there is very much a 'buyer beware' situation which you aren't warned about in a very obvious way, so it's up to you to familiarize yourself with all the 'catches'. At the back of the catalogue you will find a huge list of disclaimers about the sale in fairly small print, which you should read and make sure you know about.

Guide for Prospective Buyers

The following extract is an abbreviated version of Sotheby's *Important Information for Buyers* and does not contain certain details and references which would normally appear. This information can be found in Sotheby's sale catalogues. Similar guides can be found in all auction sale catalogues.

HOW TO BUY AT AUCTION

The following pages are designed to give you useful information on how to buy at auction. Sotheby's staff as listed at the front of this catalogue under Sales Enquiries and Information will be happy to assist you. If you have not bought at Sotheby's recently, it is important that you read the following information carefully.

PROVENANCE

In certain circumstances, Sotheby's may print in the catalogue the history of ownership of a work of art if such information contributes to scholarship or is otherwise well known and assists in distinguishing the work of art. However, the identity of the seller or previous owners may not be disclosed for a variety of reasons. For example, such information may be excluded to accommodate a seller's request for confidentiality or because the identity of prior owners is unknown given the age of the work of art.

BUYER'S PREMIUM

With the exception of Wine and Coins, a buyer's premium is payable by the buyer of each lot at a rate of 15 per cent on the first £30,000 of the hammer price of the lot and at a rate of 10 per cent on the amount by which the hammer price of the

lot exceeds £30,000. For Wine and Coins, a buyer's premium of 10 per cent of the hammer price is payable by the buyer of each lot.

VAT

Value Added Tax (VAT) may be payable on the hammer price and/or the buyer's premium. Buyer's premium may attract a charge in lieu of VAT.

1. Before the Auction

CATALOGUE SUBSCRIPTIONS AND SOTHEBY'S SEARCH SERVICES

Annual subscriptions to catalogues will ensure that you receive catalogues regularly.

PRE-SALE ESTIMATES

The pre-sale estimates are intended as a guide for prospective buyers. Any bid between the high and the low pre-sale estimates would, in our opinion, offer a fair chance of success. However, all lots, depending on the degree of competition, can realise prices either above or below the pre-sale estimates.

It is always advisable to consult us nearer the time of sale as estimates can be subject to revision. The estimates printed in the auction catalogue do not include the buyer's premium or VAT.

PRE-SALE ESTIMATES IN US DOLLARS AND EUROS

Although the sale is conducted in pounds sterling, for your convenience, the pre-sale estimates in some catalogues are also printed in US dollars and/or Euros. The rate of exchange from pound sterling to US dollar and/or Euro is the rate at the time of production of this catalogue. The rate of exchange will have changed between the time of production of the catalogue and the time of the sale. Therefore, you should not treat the estimates in US dollars or Euros as anything other than as an approximation of the estimates in pounds sterling.

CONDITION OF LOTS

Prospective buyers are encouraged to inspect the property at the pre-sale exhibitions. Solely as a convenience, Sotheby's may provide condition reports. The absence of reference to the condition of a lot in the catalogue description does not imply that the lot is free from faults or imperfections.

ELECTRICAL AND MECHANICAL GOODS

All electrical and mechanical goods are sold on the basis of their decorative value only and should not be assumed to be operative. It is essential that prior to any intended use, the electrical system is checked and approved by a qualified electrician.

2. *Bidding in the Sale*

BIDDING AT AUCTION

Bids may be executed in person by paddle during the auction, in writing prior to the sale or by telephone. All auctions are conducted in pounds sterling.

Auction speeds vary, but usually average between 50 and 120 lots per hour. The bidding steps are generally in increments of approximately 10% of the previous bid.

BIDDING IN PERSON

To bid in person at the auction, you will need to register for and collect a numbered paddle before the auction begins. Proof of identity will be required. If you have a Sotheby's Identification Card, it will facilitate the registration process.

The paddle is used to indicate your bids to the auctioneer during the sale. Should you be the successful buyer of any lot, please ensure that your paddle can be seen by the auctioneer and that it is your number that is called out. Should there be any doubts as to price or buyer, please draw the auctioneer's attention to it immediately.

All lots sold will be invoiced to the name and address in which the paddle has been registered and cannot be transferred to other names and addresses.

Please do not mislay your paddle; in the event of loss, please inform the Sales Clerk immediately. At the end of the sale, please return your paddle to the registration desk.

ABSENTEE BIDS

If you cannot attend the auction, we will be happy to execute written bids on your behalf. A bidding form can be found at the back of this catalogue. This service is free and confidential. Lots will always be bought as cheaply as is consistent with other bids, the reserves and Sotheby's commissions. In the event of identical bids, the earliest bid received will take precedence. Always indicate a 'top limit' – the hammer price to which you would bid if you were attending the auction yourself. 'Buy' and unlimited bids will not be accepted.

Telephoned absentee bids must be confirmed before the sale by letter or fax.

To ensure a satisfactory service to bidders, please ensure that we receive your bids at least 24 hours before the sale.

BIDDING BY TELEPHONE

If you cannot attend the auction, it is possible to

bid on the telephone on lots with a minimum low estimate of £1,000. As the number of telephone lines is limited, it is necessary to make arrangements for this service 24 hours before the sale.

We also suggest that you leave a maximum bid which we can execute on your behalf in the event we are unable to reach you by telephone. Multi-lingual staff are available to execute bids for you.

EMPLOYEE BIDDING

Sotheby's employees may bid in a Sotheby's auction only if the employee does not know the reserve and if the employee fully complies with Sotheby's internal rules governing employee bidding.

UN EMBARGO ON TRADE WITH IRAQ
[AS OF PUBLICATION DATE]

The United Nations trade embargo prohibits us from accepting bids from any person in Iraq (including any body controlled by Iraqi residents or companies, wherever carrying on business), or from any other person where we have reasonable cause to believe (i) that the lot(s) will be supplied or delivered to or to the order of a person in Iraq or (ii) that the lot(s) will be used for the purposes of any business carried on in or operated from Iraq. Acceptance of bids by the auctioneer is subject to this prohibition.

For further details, please contact a member of the Expert Department or the Legal Department PRIOR to bidding.

3. *The Auction*

CONDITIONS OF BUSINESS

The auction is governed by the Conditions of Business printed in this catalogue. These Condi-tions of Business apply to all aspects of the rela-tionship between Sotheby's and actual and prospective bidders and buyers. Anyone considering bidding in the auction should read them carefully. They may be amended by way of notices posted in the saleroom or by way of announcement made by the auctioneer.

CONSECUTIVE AND RESPONSIVE BIDDING

The auctioneer may open the bidding on any lot by placing a bid on behalf of the seller.

The auctioneer may further bid on behalf of the seller, up to the amount of the reserve, by placing consecutive or responsive bids for a lot.

4. *After the Auction*

PAYMENT

Payment is due immediately after the sale.

The Conditions of Business require buyers to pay immediately for their purchases. However, in limited circumstances and generally with the seller's agreement, Sotheby's may offer buyers it deems credit worthy the option of paying for their purchases on an extended payment term basis. Generally credit terms must be arranged prior to the Sale. In advance of determining whether to grant the extended payment terms, Sotheby's may require credit references and proof of identity and residence.

COLLECTION

Lots will be released to you or your authorised representative when full and cleared payment has been received by Sotheby's and a release note has been produced by our Cashiers at New Bond Street.

Smaller items can normally be collected from the Packing Room at New Bond Street, however large items will be sent to Sotheby's Kings House Warehouse.

If you are in any doubt about the location of your purchases, please contact the Sale Administrator prior to arranging collection. Removal, interest, storage and handling charges will be levied on uncollected lots.

STORAGE AND HANDLING

Storage and handling charges plus VAT may apply.

INSURANCE

Buyers are reminded that lots are only insured for a maximum of five (5) working days after the day of the auction.

DESPATCH AND TRANSIT INSURANCE

Purchases will be dispatched as soon as possible upon clearance from the Accounts Department and receipt of your written despatch instructions and of any export licence or certificates that may be required. Despatch will be arranged at the buyer's expense. Sotheby's may receive a fee for its own account from the agent arranging despatch. Estimates and information on all methods can be provided upon request and enquiries should be marked for the attention of Sotheby's Shipping Department.

Insurance cover will be arranged for property in transit unless otherwise specified in writing and will be at the buyer's expense. All shipments should be unpacked and checked on delivery and any discrepancies notified to the Transit insurer or shipper immediately.

[A form to provide shipping instructions is usually printed on the reverse of the bid slip printed in the catalogue or on the back of your buyers invoice.]

EXPORT

The export of any lot from the UK or import into any other country may be subject to one or more export or import licences being granted. It is the buyer's responsibility to obtain any relevant export or import licence. Buyers are reminded that lots purchased must be paid for immediately after the auction. The denial of any export or import licence required or any delay in obtaining such licence cannot justify the cancellation of the sale or any delay in making payment of the total amount due.

Sotheby's, upon request, may apply for a licence to export your lot(s) outside the United Kingdom.

An *EU Licence* is necessary to export from the European Community cultural goods subject to the EU Regulation on the export of cultural property (EEC No. 3911/92, Official Journal No. L395 of 31/12/92.

A *UK Licence* is necessary to move from the UK to another Member State of the EU cultural goods valued at or above the relevant UK licence limit. A *UK Licence* may also be necessary to export outside the European Community cultural goods valued at or above the relevant UK licence limit but below the EU Licence limit.

The following is a selection of some of the categories and a summary of the limits above which either an EU or a UK licence may be required for items more than 50 years old:-

Paintings in oil or tempera	£119,000
Watercolours	£23,800
Prints, Drawings & Engravings	£11,900
British Historical Portraits	£6,000
Photographs	£6,000
Arms and Armour	£20,000
Textiles	£6,000
Printed Maps	£11,900

Books	£39,600
Any Other Objects	£39,600
Manuscripts/Archives/Scale Drawings	*
Archaeological items	*

(* a licence will be required in most instances, irrespective of value)

EXPORT TO ITALY

Buyers intending to export their purchases to Italy under an Italian Temporary Cultural Import Licence are advised that the Italian authorities will require evidence of export from the UK.

ENDANGERED SPECIES

Items made of or incorporating animal material such as ivory; whale bone; tortoiseshell etc., irrespective of age or value, require a specific licence from the Department of the Environment, prior to leaving the UK. Sotheby's suggests that buyers also check with their own relevant government department regarding the importation of such items.

EMBARGO ON IMPORTATION OF PERSIAN/IRANIAN WORKS OF ART AND CARPETS IN TO THE U.S.A.

Clients considering purchasing Persian/Iranian works of art or carpets with the intention of exporting them to the U.S.A., should enquire with the relevant U.S. Government Office regarding the proper importation of such items into the U.S. prior to shipping the lot(s) to the U.S.

5. *Additional Services*

PRE-SALE AUCTION ESTIMATES

Sotheby's will be pleased to give preliminary pre-sale auction estimates for your property. This service is free of charge and is available from Sotheby's experts in New Bond Street on week days between 9 am and 4.30 pm. We advise you to make an appointment with the relevant expert department. We will inspect your property and advise you without charge. Upon request, we may also travel to your home to provide preliminary pre-sale auction estimates.

VALUATIONS

The Valuation department provides written inventories and valuations throughout Europe for many purposes including insurance, probate and succession, asset management and tax planning. Valuations can be tailored to suit most needs.

TAX AND HERITAGE ADVICE

Our Tax and Heritage department provides advice on the tax implications of sales and related legal and heritage issues. It can also assist in private treaty sales, on transfers in lieu of taxation, on the obtaining of conditional exemption from tax and on UK export issues.

Auction houses

Auction houses, country house sales and specialist sales are essentially the same thing: they are places where goods are sold under the hammer to a bidder. But there are differences in standard between them all.

Quality auction houses

At the top of the tree are the four grand ones – Phillips, Sotheby's, Bonham's and Christie's (all of which have a number of branches around the country) where you will get good-quality pieces. But the fact that these are grand establishments with often millions of pounds' worth of high-class goods for sale doesn't mean that you can't go and have a look. In fact, it's an excellent idea to wander in off Bond Street or St James's next time you are in London on a viewing day – it will be excellent practice in developing a 'good eye' for antiques because what you will see is likely to be of the best quality and will give you a yardstick when assessing pieces elsewhere. You won't always find furniture on display. Often, specialist sales are held, of anything from statues and busts to stamps or carpets, and at other times the entire 'contents' of someone's home is up for sale, and in this case there will usually be a mix of antiques and new items, as there was at the recent sale of the house contents of Elton John's manager, John Read, where there was a wonderful mix of good, original antiques, decorator-inspired pieces, modern dinner services and stylish gifts he had been given over the years, such as Lalique glass and bejewelled Swiss watches. Or perhaps the sale will consist of pop memorabilia or couturier clothing – the sale of the late Princess of Wales' designer frocks came under this type of sale (although the sale was in New York there was a viewing in London). Whatever is on sale, you will enjoy the experience and will almost certainly learn something. Again, don't be intimidated.

General salerooms

These places are very much the poor cousins of the grander antiques houses, but they bring back great memories for me. When I started 25 years ago as a dealer, I started off with general sales. They're a good place to cut your teeth and get a feel of the business if you're not looking for anything of a very high quality. But if you hunt around, there are still bargains and interesting things to be found, often as cheap as chips. For a first-time buyer I would recommend going to a local auction in a saleroom in some little market town. It

Michael 'Dick' Turpin

In the days when I was a newcomer to the business, buying modest things at sales, there was always something in my price range that I could take away. But major dealers bought the very best – Chippendale furniture, grand tapestries that I could only gawp at. These men were like the movie stars of the day – you ogled them and listened to them and paid court to them as they told their tales.

One of these was Michael Turpin. Michael, otherwise known as Dick, has a shop in central London. He has been in this business almost for ever – 40 or 50 years? It be might even more. He is recognized as one of the greatest authorities on English 18th-century furniture in the world. He is a huge imposing man with a walrus moustache and a booming voice you can hear from every corner of a saleroom, bawling out, 'That is no effing good!' Known to use more than a few swear words, he is, I think, the most charismatic larger-than-life character I have ever met. He is still in business, highly respected because he has seen it all and done it all.

I was at Christie's recently, viewing a major sale of walnut furniture and happened to bump into Dick Turpin, walking around with his lady (who, incidentally, used to work for me as my assistant in my shop in Manchester). On display were something like 20 or 30 walnut bachelor chests, as rare as hens' teeth today. Dick strolled past them all, firing off comments: 'No effing good, no effing good, no effing good, that's all right, no effing good, I remember that one in the forties: it was no effing good then and it's no effing good now!' He'd seen them all. He even knew who had repaired them in the 1920s and 1930s – good restorers who made small adjustments, experienced in working with walnut. He is typical of a type of old-fashioned dealer; if ever you want to know anything, ask Dick, because he will share his knowledge with you.

Once at a major London sale of important English furniture, where a fairly youngish auctioneer was taking his run at the rostrum, a pair of console tables came up. 'Ladies and gentlemen, Lot No 56 – a pair of 18th-century console tables.'

From the back of the room came a loud bellow: 'They're no effing good and they never were any effing good!'

The place went silent. Anybody else would have been escorted from the room unceremoniously, but the auctioneer looked up and realized it was the Governor. Obviously the sale proceeded, but notice was taken of Dick's opinion. If Dick Turpin said it was so, it was so.

On another occasion I went on to his stand at an international show in London and, showing interest, not to purchase but to admire, I commented, 'What a wonderful pair of chairs.' To which I heard the deep rumble, 'They effing ought to be. They're by the man himself – Mr Chippendale!'

Inspect, inspect, inspect!

Many years ago when I was new to the business I went to a country sale in Carmarthen. It took me a day to get there, and when I arrived I viewed everything I was interested in thoroughly, inside out and upside down. I stayed the night and was at the saleroom early the next day. Waiting for my particular lot to come along, suddenly I heard the auctioneer say. 'Ladies and gentlemen, who'll start me at £1,000 for this wonderful Victorian seven-piece salon suite?' There was a deathly hush as he scanned the room. 'OK, who'll start me at £500? I'll start on a little less. Who'll start at £200? Are there no takers? No one going to bid for this wonderful suite? Ladies and gentlemen, this is absolutely for nothing! Are you sure you're not going to bid? Who will give me £200?'

The bargain hunter in me suddenly woke up. 'Oh blimey, there's something cheap going here!' Up went my hand, *Bang* went the hammer. 'SOLD!'

It was only when I inspected the suite that I found it was riddled with woodworm. Four pieces were as spongy as Aero bars, and if you touched them they fell apart. Of the seven pieces I took three away, leaving four heaps of junk in the saleroom. From then on I never, ever, bought a piece of furniture or an object, no matter how flowery the description from the rostrum or how cheap it was. Learn from me – always inspect!

will be small, but your head won't reel from looking at too much, too soon. You will find plenty to interest you, but not so much that you can't take it all in in a couple of hours. If you are at this stage, don't even think about buying until you feel confident. Observe, learn and familiarize yourself with what might seem a frightening environment. It won't be long before you feel perfectly at ease.

Many decorators come to general sales looking for things they can tart up. For example, at a recent sale I spotted a pair of late Georgian bedposts so grey that they had obviously been out in the rain or in a leaky barn for decades. They were down for an estimated £60–£80. But someone with a keen eye knew that with a little oil and wax to restore the colour, they would be worth something. In the event, they went for £280, and I knew that the next time I saw them they would be in *Homes and Gardens* with chintz all around them.

But if you are a serious buyer I would hesitate to send you to a sale of this nature, even if you had very modest means, since it is rare to find anything of quality. I would rather send you to a nice country auction or a country house sale. Even at a grand country house there are nice pieces for reasonable prices to be found. There are a lot of trade rejects thrown into a general saleroom. Here, you will find an absolute mish-mash of goods, usually in quite a poor condition. In big cities you will often find goods that antiques dealers have been unable to sell or rejects from bigger sales. You will find the contents of modest homes up for grabs. Now and then, you might spot something special that has slipped though the net. But I should add that the last time I was at Christie's general goods saleroom in South Kensington, I spotted a runner – and if he was there, you can bet that others, too, were likely to be there during the course of the preview. Nothing much of any worth would escape their eagle eyes for a hopeful novice to snap up.

I have seen some remarkable things in salerooms where pieces have been underestimated by the auctioneer. At one country sale, an old woman put her treasured walnut Queen Anne bureau bookcase up for sale. She had just sold her little terraced cottage for about £10,000 and was convinced that a piece of furniture must be worth proportionately less. As the bidding started and bids for the bookcase rose, someone had to get her a hardback chair and a glass of water because she nearly fainted. When it went for £14,000 under the hammer I think she did swoon. All the other chattels in the house were ordinary cottagey bits and pieces, but her parents had worked in a grand country house and had been given the Queen Anne piece after 40 years' service. Today, of course, the value of such a bookcase could be over £50,000, but it's all relative – how many terraced cottages can you still buy for £10,000?

Country house sales

There was a time in the fifties and sixties when grand country houses and stately homes were being emptied and pulled down by the dozens every year and their contents sold for a song. That was the time to buy, and I suspect that many people did, often buying massive pieces that would have looked wonderful in rooms 18.5m (60ft) long and 4.5m (15ft) high, but were impossible to fit in their more modest homes. As a result, sadly, many pieces were hacked down and cut to fit. Magnificent Georgian bureau-bookcases lost their top halves; bookcases and wardrobes lost their ornate pediments; tall boys became lowboys, and leaves of fine mahogany tables were discarded and chopped up to make bookshelves or even – horrors – firewood!

Country house sales might have passed their manic heyday, but there are still plenty of them to be found, giving us all a chance to poke around in another world and perhaps dream a little. They are a glamorous environment and can provide a wonderful day out with an added opportunity to buy a small slice of history. Country house sales come in all styles and sizes, from the very grand, such as Luton Hoo, Bedfordshire, which was recently on the market, lock, stock and barrel, or Eaton Hall, the Duke of Westminster's former stately pile when the Duke, the richest landowner in England, built a smaller, more modern house in the grounds of the old one. Whatever the reason for the sale of the contents, you will often see merchandise collected over many hundreds of years, over many generations. The ambience is very special and it sometimes drives people into giving £200 or £300 for a 1930s electric fire! We call that particular madness 'country house fever' and I have to admit that even dealers have been known to succumb to it, so beguiling is the sense of history and romance of the setting, particularly on a lazy summer's day when the scent of roses and hay meadows drifts in through open windows and the rooms smell of centuries of beeswax.

One of the earliest country house sales I attended was in Yorkshire at a marvellous place, Old Brabham Hall, where there was a wide selection of things, from the grand down to the very ordinary. At the viewing, I spotted a pair of decanters of exquisite quality, etched with the Prince of Wales' feathers. The estimate of £200–£300 was within my price range and I thought they were special, so I started to go into the bidding. Suddenly it was up to £500, then £600. Long after I had dropped out, canny dealers kept going and going, ever upwards; finally, the decanters went for £3,000, a huge sum over 20 years ago. Older dealers with more experience knew what I wasn't aware of: these decanters were by a specific glassmaker and had belonged to the Prince of Wales, who had given them to a member of the family. I was told there were known to be just four pairs in existence, the Queen having the other three pairs.

Sadly we will never see the likes again of some of the sales I've been to. I honestly think I witnessed the passing of an era. I recall going to a sale on the Scottish borders of Lord Dalhousie's possessions. He had been the viceroy of India in the later part of the 19th century and had amassed a treasure trove of collectables – the mind-blowing collection of things that were there will never be seen again gathered under one roof. There were even copies of Tipu's throne carved in wood in Indian workshops and gilded – the original was in gold – and Tipu's infamous beheading sword.

Rupert Spencer
— AN OLD FASHIONED AUCTIONEER

In the Yorkshire area a local firm, Henry Spencer, used to hold some wonderful country house sales as grand house after house tumbled to taxes and deaths, marking the end of dynasties. The auctioneer was Rupert Spencer, an elderly man when I started in the business, a real old-fashioned auctioneer and great charmer. He'd get up on to the rostrum at about five to ten on the nail, and welcome everybody. 'Ladies and gentlemen, we are about to start this dispersal sale of the so-and-so family at such-and-such hall which has been the family's home for 300 years. I would like to welcome here this morning Mr John Phillips from Bond Street, Mr Arnold Singer from Mayfair, Mr So-and-So from Mallets over there' – all illustrious dealers of some standing. He would go through the list, and then he'd start on the local regular private buyers: 'Mr and Mrs Silver, how nice to see you again – I hope you take away something wonderful from the sale today.' He would go on to say, 'I've checked with Reuters this morning and there is only one Hindu altar being sold in this country today.' Finally, he would say, quoting Keats: 'Ladies and gentlemen, spend your money wisely, buy the best objects you can, and always remember a thing of beauty is a joy for ever! It's ten o'clock and let's start the sale with Lot No. 1!"

Some of the grand places where sales were held were the homes of military families going back some 200 or 300 years. From tours of duty all over the world, to India, China, Africa, members of the family had brought back furniture and objects the likes of which you'll never see again. I remember once seeing a framed flag in one of those country houses that was the very one removed from the Summer Palace in Peking during the Boxer Rebellion.

Going to a country house sale

Country house sales are advertised well in advance in many of the more upmarket Sunday newspapers, glossy magazines such as *Country Life* or *Homes and Gardens* as well as in the trade press. It is always advisable to send off for a catalogue, because not only will it give you a detailed inventory of what is for sale, but it will also give you an estimated price guide, and it will save you from wasting your time if you are looking for a particular object like a garden statue or an oak settle.

A smashing day out can be had at a country house sale, whether planned in advance or done on the spur of the moment. It may be sunny and bright, but however relaxing the atmosphere, be sure not to leave your wits under the arbour.

Sometimes, you might be on holiday or on a drive in the country when you see signs or posters directing you to a sale. Many people decide on impulse to a visit to such a sale and go with no intention of buying – they just want a nice drive with an interesting destination and a good look at how the wealthy live. But beware, you need a strong will not to bid for something or another in the heat of the moment.

Whether you are buying or not, my advice to you would be to get to the sale the day before, if it is local; or even consider staying overnight in the village pub or some nice bed and breakfast so that you can make a thorough inspection of the goods at a leisurely pace. On the day of the sale, even if you get there the moment the gates are opened, there will almost certainly be so many other people crammed in that you will find it almost impossible to inspect the goods.

Take a floor plan of your house and the dimensions of all your rooms and of furniture already in those rooms that you want to keep. Something in a grand house with panelled walls and acres of polished floorboards can look charming and quite petite, but once you've got it home it can be a real white elephant, and as big as one.

Have some idea of what you want, and never, ever, buy on the spur of the

moment unless the lot you can't resist is going for just for a pound or two, because the chances are that you won't know what to do with three torn leather poufs and a stuffed squirrel under a cracked bell jar.

Remember, if you intend to bid, that you must register, so that the auctioneer will know you are a serious buyer. Usually, registering will include giving your name, address and telephone number and proposed method of payment should your bid be lucky. You should also enquire how much is the buyer's premium or 'commission', As with auctions, you must also arrange for the removal of your goods within a certain period of time (usually 24 hours); otherwise you will be charged storage. The auctioneer can help you with this if necessary.

Values and prices change according to the mood and market. Recently, I was at the preview of the house contents of a famous and very wealthy person and was surprised at how modest the estimated prices were for most of the more decorative items. You could have bought top-quality glass, silver and leather goods and some nicely framed prints for less than £100. This reflected the slightly cautious mood in the market and also, changes in fashion. Many of the items were quite flamboyant at a time when interior designers have decreed that the minimalist look is in. Two years before these items would have been fiercely contested and the estimates would have taken that into account.

If you are a serious buyer but everything inside the house is way beyond your means, get out into the outbuildings. Have a thorough scour around, because sometimes in these great houses a lot of nice but broken things were discarded to the stables or old wash-houses and a little judicious repair could be all that something needs.

If you find something like this inspect the piece carefully and use your common sense to judge whether it is broken beyond repair. Is it so spongy and riddled with woodworm that you can push your finger into the wood? If it's a chair, is the back broken, or if it's a table, does it have only three legs? Has the walnut veneer lifted or bubbled where someone has watered a pot plant? If it's a cupboard, are the hinges broken, are the jambs split? Does a Georgian card table gape and 'smile' at you? Is a Sèvres porcelain vase badly cracked; has that Wedgwood teapot lost its spout and lid? You have to ask yourself 'when does an original turn into a liquorice allsort (see page 183)? If there are any obvious, major faults, walk away. The cost of restoration will be far too much.

Once I went to a sale in Parr in Cornwall, at the type of house where you went down a driveway that went for about 5.5km (3½ miles) through a park full of deer grazing under mature trees hundreds of years old. In the house each room had a mixture of furniture from Georgian right back to Elizabethan and about 1500 when the family was first established, and displayed wonderfully exotic things they had brought back from all over the world as they flourished and ruled all the pink patches on the old atlases. On the staircase from top to bottom were portraits of ancestors, finishing at the bottom with an 18-year-old first lieutenant who had died at the Battle of the Somme, the last of the male line. It was his sister who had passed away; and the contents were being sold by Cornwall County Council, who had inherited everything, all that history, in the old lady's will, and were turning the house into an old people's home.

I walked into the dining room and there was an oil painting that must have been 4.5m (14ft) long, depicting the Battle of the Nile in the 18th century, in the forefront of which was one of the ancestors I'd seen on the staircase wall, the Admiral Saul Gravesaul, who was number two to Nelson at the battle. There were items in the family collection, such as a bosun's whistle, given as a present by Nelson to the Admiral and trophies taken round the world. These wonderful exciting contents were to be dispersed and would be gone for ever. I was there at the dismantling of something like 400 years of military and naval history, the sale of trophies taken from battles and naval engagements and relics of one extinct family's time in high office.

In those days there were such exciting things to buy. You could wander into an outbuilding and who knew what you might find in the bottom of a croquet box?

The private house sale

I have been to many sales in quite modest homes, where, perhaps following the death of a well-loved parent, the heirs decide to sell everything and split the proceeds. Sometimes farmers die and their possessions are sold because they have no heir to follow them; or, in these hard times, farmers might go bankrupt and there's a sale where everything is up for grabs, including the cows, the pigs, the milk churns and the tractors. In such cases, you might be lucky and discover that the house or farm, however humble, has been in the family for generations, and that there are some charming, original antiques just waiting to be discovered. Hotels, especially country-house hotels, for which there was a fad in the eighties, are other places where total contents are often sold.

BABIES FOR SALE

FOR A TELEVISION SERIES I was making, I helped Jim and Annice, a keen couple who collect bisque piano babies, to find two more perfect examples to add to their large collection.

Bisque is a type of porcelain with a matt or biscuit finish and the pieces known as piano babies are very cute, like Lucy Atwell dolls (another collectors' area). They are called piano babies because people used to place them on the top of pianos. Because they are so charming, they have become almost as rare as hens' teeth and quite expensive. When I was asked to find a sale to film for a programme, I decided to use one of my runners to look out for any forthcoming sales where piano babies might be found. He came up trumps with an obscure little sale in the Midlands.

WHEN WE ARRIVED the day before the sale in time for the viewing and my friends saw rusty washing machines stacked up with old beds and lawnmowers, I think they thought I was out of my mind and prepared to beat a hasty retreat. They calmed down when they saw a treasure trove, right at the front, of some dozen piano babies – obviously some local person's personal collection. (This is a good tip: if you're looking for smaller and more valuable items at a general sale, don't be put off by the everyday junk you will find. Head straight for the rostrum where the auctioneer will sit, which is where such things are likely to be.) Few people were in evidence at the viewing, and, even better, I could see no dealers hovering around the table as you might expect when rare items come up.

FOR BISQUE I use the teeth test: that is, I gently rub the piece with the enamel on my front teeth to get the 'feel' of it. Don't bite it whatever you do. Genuine bisque has a sandy, very hard finish to the glaze. A repair feels smooth and almost plasticky, and when it's fired at a later date, it's never possible to achieve the same heat of the original firing. That's why the original is called bisque – it's cooked like a dry biscuit. A little restoration is acceptable, but not too much . On inspection one of the babies proved to have been badly damaged and an entire leg had been replaced – that wasn't acceptable. Another, a beach baby with bucket and spade, had lost it's original bucket, but that's acceptable. A couple had quite ugly features. But there were two that were about as perfect and as cute as you could hope to find.

'WE'LL GO FOR BOTH,' my friends decided.

'NOW, HOW MUCH are you prepared to bid for them?' I asked. They looked in the catalogue and Jim was shocked. Last time he had bought, some years ago, the babies had cost him 'washers', which was his way of saying loose change. According to him, his entire collection didn't cost as much as the estimate for just one of the babies.

'MAYBE, but all of your collection will be worth much more than washers by now,' I reminded him. 'And how often does one of these babies, let alone a herd of them, come up for sale?'

'NEVER,' he had to concede.

THEY WERE LUCKY – they bought the babies for spot on the estimated price. If we had gone to a specialist sale those bisque pieces would have gone for double at least.

Such sales are usually advertised in local newspapers. It is only worth spending money for national advertising for the grander country house sales. Many farm sales are advertised on posters nailed to trees around the farm, so if you are out for a drive, you could keep a sharp eye out. I would advise against just 'dropping in' on the actual day of the sale because you will never have time to inspect the goods and ten to one you will be caught up in auction fever. However, if a small sale is advertised in your area it is well worth going along the day before to inspect the goods because you will find that usually only local people will attend the sale and you won't be competing against high flyers and dealers from all over the country. But bear in mind that anything of local or county interest, such as a painting of a local view or a piece of memorabilia relating to a well-known character from those parts, will excite a lot of local interest and will fetch quite a high price.

Recently, I attended a sale in a handsome little farmhouse with a couple who were looking for a large painting or some prints to fill a space on the sitting-room wall of their Victorian house. I found the sale advertised in the trade press within an easy drive, allowing us time to go the day before to inspect, and I'm glad that we did, because on the actual day of the sale the place was packed. It was a small local sale, so few dealers came, which can always help to keep prices down. The couple were quite taken with some regional maps and scenes and I advised them that in this case local interest would push the prices very high, as it did. Instead they ended up by buying some delightful signed lithographs by John Leitch, the cartoonist who worked for *Punch*, which were totally in keeping with their room and with the other engravings already on the walls, and were well within the estimated price. I have no doubt that had these particular cartoons been in a major specialist sale in one of the big auction houses they would have gone for a lot more. I tell this story because it's important to know if there is any local connection with some piece you are anxious to buy and set your bid accordingly.

Specialist collectors' auctions

Specialist sales for collectors now make up 50 per cent of all auctions. If you're trying to build up a collection of certain items, you will quickly become an expert at knowing where to look and, by getting a specialist magazine or newsletter from other collectors, you will hear of any upcoming sales. For example, there are big Beatles fairs and conventions several times a

BUDGETING

THE FOLLOWING STORY of a trip to a specialist sale is a good example of when it's best to apply the rule having a budget and sticking to it.

Jane, who was landscaping her garden, was looking for an architectural piece to make a statement and as a focal point in a patio area, where she intended holding small garden parties and wine tastings in her business as a wine seller. She decided that, out of her quite substantial overall budget for her landscaping, she could spend £600–£800 on a feature piece, which seemed reasonable for a statue or a large urn.

By looking through the trade press, I discovered a specialist sale of garden furniture and related architectural pieces in Edinburgh. It was a long way to go, but as I have said before, antiques hunting can be fun. You can have a nice outing or a mini-break and see a bit of the country. I sent off for the catalogue and we looked through it before we left. Many of the pieces were more expensive than Jane could afford, but there were one or two nice ones with a wine theme, so she decided to attend the sale despite the distance.

It's a good thing we went in person and didn't put in a phone bid because one of the pieces that had attracted her eye, a grape press, turned out to be far smaller than it looked in the catalogue. In fact, I was sure that it wasn't a grape press at all, but the bottom half of something or other. Several stunning garden seats were rejected because the estimates were far too high. Then Jane came across a pair of elegant, wrought-iron gates. She had not previously considered these as a feature when we went through the catalogue, but in the flesh, they were stylish and within her budget. 'They're perfect!' she enthused. 'I'll go for them.'

I told her that if she got them, she should leave them exactly as they were, encrustations and all, and certainly she should not attempt to 'restore' them with a lick of shiny whiter-than-white paint. And then I murmured a word of caution: 'They are Regency or early Victorian. There will be a lot of people and dealers bidding for them, so if the price starts to escalate, *stick to your budget, but don't lose them for a bid.*'

It turned out that this was good advice. The gates went for £1,700 to another bidder – well over £2,300 with the commission, VAT and transport. Now, someone of less steely backbone might have been so keen to buy something after going all that way that he would have cast caution to the winds and bid wildly, ending up with something that broke his budget. It's true that sometimes hesitation can bring disappointment, but spending more than you intended can be depressing.

Yes, it was disappointing to return home empty-handed. But, as Jane told me, she had enjoyed the experience of an auction, she had learned a great deal, and she was determined to keep looking.

And that, in a nutshell is what antiques hunting is all about: the thrill of the chase, the enjoyment of the day, looking, learning, not losing your head and wanting to continue through the many disappointments along the way, and what you will end up with are some lovely pieces in your home that will give you years of pleasure.

year, not just in this country but also in Europe and the United States, where collectors sell and trade. But it will quickly be obvious that at any place where ardent collectors go there will be strong competition and prices will reflect this.

Recently I went with Olga and Olga, a mother and daughter, to buy an Oriental rug. What we call Oriental carpets covers Turkish, Afghan, Armenian, Chinese and of course, Persian carpets. Usually they have a pile, even if it is a shaved one. Not all valuable carpets are Oriental: the Europeans created their own, flatter-woven carpets which are more like tapestry, such as Aubusson ones from France, which are renowned for their flower designs and soft, pastel colours.

Carpets are not a specialist area of mine, but by talking to rug and carpet dealers with a lifetime experience I was able to glean the state of the market; and the in-house expert was on hand to offer advice. I said to him, 'This is not really my field. Am I right in thinking that the best example in terms of wear, tear, colour and quality, will bring the best price, and is that the best way to go?' He replied, 'Yes, David. Exactly the same rule applies as in furniture. Look for the best example.'

Carpets get worn, and you should look for the one in the best condition. Colour is important, as is design. If you can't afford the one you've decided is the best, buy the best you can within your budget. If it's the case that the best you can afford is slightly smaller than the size you wanted, then buy a slightly smaller one. Cut your cloth down to size. Just because you want something big, don't buy something second rate.

While all auction sales are conducted in exactly the same way – the viewing, the registration, the bid – there are little flourishes that belong to certain specialist areas. With a carpet sale you will walk in and find that it looks like a Turkish bazaar, with hundreds of carpets of every size hanging from the walls and the bigger ones piled up in sofa-high heaps in the centre of the floor. Now you would be quite right in asking, 'How on earth can I see the carpets at the bottom of the pile?' Don't worry – four times a day there is an event called the turning of the carpets, when saleroom porters line up (very much like the centre court tarpaulin pullers at Wimbledon when it rains) and move the carpets from one heap to another; and what was on the top now goes to the bottom. Find out the times of the turning and be there to watch, or else you might miss something crucial, While the porters are doing the turning, you can stand there armed with a catalogue and make some scribbled notes. If you want to inspect any carpet while they are being turned, simply ask them to pause while you have a careful look.

When I went to the sale with my clients Olga and Olga they had looked at the catalogue and decided that they were keen on a certain very large rug that happened to be at the bottom of the pile. When they came to inspect it, they found that there was a huge hole in the middle. It so happened that we found that at this time traditional designs, such as Persian rugs with wonderful intricate patterns and highly colourful woven rugs, are not that fashionable because of the interior designer business – predominantly in America and in Europe – pushing the market-place to a minimalist look. The prices of oriental carpets and rugs reflect trends in decorating, so this proved to be one of the occasions when what I call 'the curse of the designer' can work for the buyer. Much to their pleasure and surprise, the two Olgas were able to get the rug of their dreams for £400, probably a tenth of what it might have cost a year or two back. They were so delighted that they bought two rugs; but I should point out that they didn't buy the second on a whim – they had previously inspected it.

What goes around comes around, and sooner or later a particular look – in this case, the traditional carpet – will come back again and the price will soar. I think the same is probably so with furniture and with certain objects of art, which also become fashionable, or go out of fashion through interior decorators, designers and magazines, all showing the public what's 'in', rather as fashion designers state that this year's colour is grey or pink.

chapter 5

The Restoration Game

Some antiques buyers, especially if, like dealers, they plan to sell on what they buy, are obsessed with restoration. They buy splinters and glue them together; they repaint a flaky picture so that only an X-ray could reveal the original artist's brush strokes.

There is no doubt that restoration has its place in preserving history. The better the example, the more original it is, the better off you'll be owning it, and in many cases there is nothing wrong with restoration as long as it is not overdone. You can even enhance something by restoring it, as with the long-case clock example on page 120; but there comes a time when you can over-restore something and ruin it. And restoration can affect artistic integrity, in the case of paintings, for instance. More and more, museums and art galleries are finding it unacceptable to fake a repair. Today, if a painting has large gaps where the paint has flaked off or been destroyed by water damage, curators prefer to indicate with the lightest of touches what the missing spaces would have looked like. To hire a counterfeiter to paint in the gaps so that you can't tell the difference between the work of the original artist and the counterfeiter's is artistically dishonest. If you are doing it to be able to fetch a higher price, then it is fraudulent. The question is: where do you draw the line between what is reasonable and acceptable and what not?

To restore or not?

There has to be a degree of common sense applied to the subject of restoration and repair. No one would suggest throwing a broken Chippendale chair on to a bonfire or discarding a Sheraton marquetry table with much of the inlay missing, so yes, in such cases, you hire the best restorers available and get them to repair the piece so beautifully that only an expert can tell the difference. You can't use a table with a leg missing, a dressing table with a cracked mirror or a chair with stained and ripped upholstery, so, unless it's going to relegated to the attic forever, repair is the only way forward. If the damage is bad and the repairs extensive the value will be greatly reduced, but at least the piece remains in use and you can get some benefit and pleasure from it.

With less valuable and rare pieces the cost of restoration can far outweigh the value of the piece – this is true particularly with glass or china. With a piece of furniture often the only thing to do is either to completely rebuild it in as economical a way as possible or to cannibalize it, using the nicely aged wood and related parts to repair something worthwhile. If it is broken glass, often the least troublesome solution is to throw it away. I am sure many people will gasp with horror at this, but the fact that something is old does not make it sacred. There are some pretty awful bit and pieces in circulation that are far past their useful life, yet they seem to go round and round the salerooms for ever, hanging around like the ancient mariner. They would be better disposed of.

Furniture is not the only area where some judicious restoring can make a difference. A barometer, for example, is a working instrument. If one has been unrestored, and untouched since 1780 it goes without saying that when you buy it, it will probably not be working; but the working of the instrument is a fundamental thing that it may well be possible to rectify. If you open the back, you will almost certainly find that the interior is encrusted with dirt and cobwebs. None of that matters. What is important is the condition of the tube. Is it unbroken with mercury still in it? You might find that the tube is intact but is full of bubbles and that's why it doesn't work. Take it to a specialist restorer. He will take the mercury out, clean the tube and replace it. He will clean, oil and regulate the workings and it will be as good as new.

The same applies to clocks or watches. It is hard to find a fine antique clock that has survived in its original condition after a century or two of handling and winding up. If you are fortunate enough to own, inherit or buy a fine old clock, a certain amount of restoration is acceptable. If you know nothing about it and do some research you might increase its value, and that alone might pay for any cleaning and restoration. You never know, your research might reveal that the piece that has been ticking away on the family mantel shelf forever is another Thomas Tompion. Ten years ago two of his clocks, a night miniature long-case clock and a Charles II *grande sonnerie* ebony bracket clock, respectively made £880,000 and £352,000 at Christie's.

To restore or not is really a matter of picking things that you feel have the quality to make it worthwhile and the ability to make a judgement will come with knowledge and experience. As a dealer, I have to consider if there will be any mileage in restoring a piece. Not just so that I make a profit, but also so the client I sell it to will have something that will enhance in value while he or she has it. Of course you want to make money, but you also want to give good deals as well. The better pieces you buy and the better deal you do for a client, the more you establish yourself as reliable, and as a result they will come back to you time and time again.

The piano

It was an ebonized wood and gilt grand piano. When I first inspected it before a sale at a big London auction house, I saw that the case needed quite a lot of restoration and it played dud notes, which meant there was quite a lot wrong with the innards, but nevertheless I immediately recognized it as wonderful quality. It was down in the catalogue as having come from a Continental dealer with a strong estimate against it. I bid for it along with a few other dealers, but it didn't make its reserve price and was 'bought in' (see page 182).

Before I left the saleroom, I had another glance at the piano, which reinforced my opinion that it was a corker. The case was in a nice original condition but some odd bits of inlay, the ivory decoration, had fallen out – which I knew would be easy to replace. I decided to do a little homework to see if I could somehow acquire and repair it without breaking the bank, in order to get it to a state where I could resell it in perfect condition and as a fully working musical instrument.

From my own experience I knew approximately how much it might cost to restore the case. The movement – the internal mechanism of the piano – was an area where I would need specialist expertise. I had many questions that I needed to have answered, so I did what I always advise people to do: I looked for a source to advise me.

I went to someone who was recommended to me, a tuner-cum-restorer and asked what his fee was to have a look. He quoted me £70, which was very reasonable, so I told him to give me a condition report.

He ran his eye over the piano that evening and telephoned me. Some of the strings were corroded and should be replaced. But the main problem, he said, were that the pegs that held the wires into the frame were loose and also needed to be replaced. Unless they were, it would be impossible to get any tension on the wires and the piano would never play a tune. Also, it needed to be rebushed.

'Can it be done?' I asked.

'No problem,' was his reply.

'How much will it cost?' I asked.

He said a couple of thousand pounds would get the piece restrung, rebushed, with new pegs. But it so happened that I knew a more local man who has done 17 years' tuning and restoration, and he said he could do it for less, which sounded pretty good to me. I was quite happy to spend £1,500 on the case itself. The instrument had been made by a medal-winning firm that made top-quality instruments, and had a good history and provenance.

I knew that the piano had been shipped over from the Continent by a dealer who would be most reluctant to go to the trouble of shipping it back. Returning to the auctioneers, I put in a keen offer. They conferred with their vendor, and after much haggling we came to a price. By now, I knew the value of the piano and the cost of repairs, so at this point it became a poker game.

Restoration would give me a case in wonderful condition and a movement that was totally rejuvenated, restrung and cleaned. From a poorly presented piece for which nobody was prepared to bid very much at auction, I would possess something that was worth more than it had cost me. (Ultimately, the total restoration cost was three times my estimate but it turned out to be worth it.)

The icing on the cake was the wonderful history of the piano. It was made for Napoleon III for his private apartments. The maker was a well-known French company who made pianos for the royal heads in Europe, including Isabel of Spain and Queen Victoria. I found that there are some examples of similar pianos to be found today in the Queen's Royal Collection; I wasn't sure at which royal residence they were, but if I made some enquiries I would discover easily enough information that would give the provenance an added cachet. The company exhibited at major exhibitions from 1851 to 1860. It would not be hard to get catalogues from specialist booksellers I know, which would tell me what they exhibited and where. I would be able lay all this evidence before a prospective client in order to persuade him to buy what was, in reality, a very valuable piece and a fine investment.

I was able to see the potential in that piano and act upon it because of my experience, knowledge and contacts. In a smaller way, you can do the same by using your eyes, your brain and your enterprise. The most important thing, if you happen to spot something going very reasonably that you think is worth restoring, is to do your homework before rushing in to make an offer because, and I keep saying it, some things simply aren't worth the candle.

The Irish state bed disaster

This story of another restoration is an example of failing to realize that something that seemed a potentially wonderful buy wasn't, because I didn't take stock before I wrote the cheque. It is also another example of how you should look at all aspects of an antique before buying, see what needs to be done to it and, if it is an unfamiliar field, seek advice.

In the 1980s I saw a huge 1840s Irish state bed in a friend's warehouse in the north of England and, despite its sadly tattered condition, was so taken with it that I immediately bought it for an astounding £11,000, without stopping to think. Originally it would have been 4.25–4.5m (14–15ft), made for a stately home with a 5.5m (18ft) ceiling. Now it was about 3.6m (12ft) tall, the posts having been reduced for a smaller room. It was slightly dumpy, but the style and size were still grand and, with four-poster beds being 'in', I thought it would sell like hot cakes. I felt I was experienced with most aspects of furniture restoration, so it never occurred to me that I was about to get into deep water with an upholstery problem.

The pine superstructure of the bed was completely covered in antique silk velvet, which was hanging off it in strips. I took it to my restorer, who took off all the perished silk and telephoned me with the ominous words: 'I think you'd better come around and have a look at this.'

When I got there I was horrified to see what I can only describe as a pile of scrap Georgian pine lying in a heap. When my restorer had stripped off the silk, he had taken it down to the basic pine construction, revealing the fact that the huge cast-iron wormscrew bolts were loose and the wooden bushes needed to be relined. I thought, 'I've got £11,000 involved in this heap of kindling.' I had no choice but to tell him to get on with the work.

I had another terrible shock when I went to see my upholsterer, who informed me that the job would be unbelievably costly. It was a major job. He pointed out that all the silk velvet would have to be laid down on top of the pine, stretched and glued. All the pile would have to go one way, and so there would be a lot of wastage. Something else I hadn't anticipated was the

cost of the original type of silk velvet, which could still be bought in Paris. I almost fainted when I was told it was £200 a metre and 100 metres would be needed.

Eventually I had to settle for a very short-pile cotton velvet, but even that cost a great deal of money. I had wonderful crewel-work curtains made; these were also very expensive, but at that stage there is no point in skimping on the finishing touches. The total bill for the restoration was about £12,000, which meant that, including the initial cost, I had forked out £23,000 in total. It was 18 months before I found a buyer, a regular client of mine who knocked me down to £19,000.

So not all my buys are winners. In this case, although the bed was magnificent, I hadn't taken enough time to consider what needed to be spent on it.

A small long-case clock

There are times when restoration is more costly than you've anticipated, but it is worth the extra cost. This was the case when recently, I helped a couple put the heartbeat into their charming Lakeland cottage. They had called me in to advise them about purchasing a long-case clock that would sit nicely next to the stone fireplace and also fit under the exposed beams. I told them that what would fit into their room like a glove, on their budget of £1,000 plus restoration costs, would be a nice, simple oak clock by someone like a local Kendal clockmaker. Since there was a limit to height, they should look for a 30-hour clock, which winds with a rope or a chain and is smaller than other types of clock because the weights go down to the floor. An eight-day clock has a longer trunk because of the space, which is needed for the weights to go down.

Good-quality 30-hour clocks of a smaller height are hard to find. I checked the trade papers and marked out three or four possible sales and rang them to enquire if they had a clock of the right dimensions. I found one at a sale that sounded promising and we decided that we would go down to view it – or as they say in the trade, 'give it a coat of looking at'.

I think the couple were envisioning a handsome mahogany clock with a pagoda top, but apart from the fact that such a clock would be too big, the style would be entirely wrong for a country cottage. There is no rigid rule about mahogany for town and oak or pine for the country; you can mix and match furniture. But I think that some pieces look and feel right in certain environments and others just look wrong.

The most important thing to remember, however, is that a clock isn't just a piece of furniture: it has to work. Restoring neglected clocks can cost a fortune, so always get expert advice about the condition before you buy. Clocks have three important parts: the case, the dial or the face and the movement or internal mechanism.

It's always important to get an original dial, and watch out for clocks that are 'marriages' of parts that don't belong together. Clock owners through the ages have often changed the cases and the mechanism to make them more fashionable. Some repair or replacement is wear or tear, but even so it does affect the value.

The sale was 250 miles away at Oxford, but as I tell people, you can't rely on the catalogue: if you want to find the kit you must always be prepared to travel. It was worth the journey – there were plenty of clocks, but the state of some of them proved to me that you have to go to a viewing in person. One that looked promising showed a tell-tale trail of fresh dust indicating that there were woodworm that were still alive and kicking; some areas were so spongy with flight holes that you could push your finger through them – a restorer's nightmare. Now I know the word 'woodworm' strikes fear into most people, but as long as the infestation is not too much, it's not a problem, as it can be treated. However, a piece of timber that looks like an Aero bar and crushes under your finger, you have to avoid like the plague.

The clock we had come to see looked exactly right. I looked over the case, which was signed by the maker, 'Edward Hallam of Lutterworth'. Quite a lot of dentil moulding (moulding that looks like teeth, or the top of a castle wall) had been knocked off the top over the years. The hood had had a knock, causing the clock itself to slip down inside a fraction. The face and chaptering (the divisions or numerals) needed resilvering and you could tell that the seconds finger was a replacement because the original would have been blued. All these points were simple ones for a restorer to attend to.

The estimate in the catalogue was £200–£500, very modest for a clock like this. I had to tell the couple that as this was a country clock selling in a country district, there would be a lot of competition on the day. I suspected it would go for closer to £1,000 and that they'd better start checking the piggy bank because restoration would not come cheap. The question was, would they beat the trade and would they stay within their budget?

It was important to know how much restoration would cost; there would be no point in bidding if that was going to be way beyond their means. We checked this out and got a quote of about £900. This could be very tight. But it was within their budget so they knew they could go ahead and bid.

They bought the clock for £1,250. With commission, VAT, transport back to the Lake District and restoration, their total expenditure was close on £3,000. The clock had broken the bank, but they thought it was worth it when they saw it ticking away by the fireplace.

Knowing when not to bother

Sometimes you have to realize that something – and this is particularly so with mechanical things – can never be restored. There is a point where I, as a dealer, will look at it and think, 'It's in a very bad condition. You don't want to know about it. There are nasty breaks. They can all be repaired but how much will it cost?'

I have a mental scale of 0–10 with everything I inspect and it's a good idea for you to do the same. When I look at a really battered piece my thoughts are that it has gone to the bottom of the scale. It is true that it can always be restored. Everything can be restored, whatever the level of damage. Say that it's fairly riddled with woodworm. It could be filled, whole chunks of wood could be replaced, but what have you got left at the end of the day? Certainly not an original antique. It's more likely that you've got something that is so over-restored that it will never be considered as a really nice example and would therefore be very hard to re-sell. And how much would it cost? Probably too much. In cases like this, no matter how much you want it, walk away.

Another good example of pieces for which it's best not to attempt restoration is smiling tables. Suppose you've always wanted a Regency card table but they are wildly expensive and you can't afford one yet. Then you spot one in an auction catalogue you have sent away for and the estimated price is astonishing low, well within your pocket. You go to check it out and at once you notice it because it's smiling at you – in fact, it isn't only smiling, it's yawning. By that, I mean that the top leaf that folds down doesn't lie flat. It is warped.

You give the piece a thorough going-over. The wood is a lovely rich mahogany, the veneer is thick, the legs are the right shape. Only the baize looks new, but that's to be expected in a piece this age. It's perfect in every way, except for its smile. What do you do? If you have any sense, you'll walk away.

To buy an article like that will lead to amazing problems. It can be put back to its original state but to do so is a major restoration job. The restorer must take the whole guts out of the table to straighten it. The only way of doing that is by taking the veneers off both sides of the top then milling out a certain amount of the main body of the table. Next, a piece of marine ply is usually put into it. It is reinforced so that the tension is pulled back in; then all the veneer is replaced and it's put into a press with glue and straightened. So inside that wonderful antique table is marine ply and glue. It is not visible of course, but you've had to go through a butchering process to do it.

Degrees of restoration

It's funny but dealers, particularly picture dealers, love dirt. When going to an auction they are delighted when they see an untouched, dirty, even filthy picture with years of nicotine, grime and soot. A broken, smashed frame, too? Great! Dealers love antiques in that original, untouched condition. They vie with each other, and fight to buy them.

They buy that picture for a large sum and they have the frame restored, or replaced with another frame. Like most pictures, it needs re-lining; and they have it cleaned and re-glazed, re-varnished until the painting is revealed, crystal-clear in all its original colours. Then they put it back into an auction. The same men who were competing for it before don't want to know. The picture is withdrawn and sold privately to a buyer who wants it looking new.

The reason for this is that dealers are treasure hunters or gold miners at heart. But their idea of treasure is not money but what they call 'new untouched goods'. They don't really want restored goods and yet they like to restore. Dealers tell me that they'd be better off financially taking that picture and reversing the cycle. Put it back into an old dirty smashed frame, perhaps kill off the varnish, and the same people would fight for it again.

I'm no different from the rest. I walk into a saleroom and I see a desk. It's been re-leathered, it's been polished, it's been cleaned. Perhaps the restoration may not be sympathetic enough for me, or – it doesn't appeal to me. The point here is that, like many dealers, I want to restore it to my standards. If I were to buy a similar desk in its unrestored state I would take it to my restorer and tell him to save the leather. He would clean and wax the wood and then replace the original leather. You don't want to walk in and see a brand new sparkling leather with clean tooling jumping at you. If it's shot completely and torn, he would replace it with a new one which, after careful application, will look as sympathetic as possible to the piece of furniture. In fact, my restorer could play around for three or four days with a leather, and when he's finished with it, you would find it very difficult to know it's not an old leather. This is not cheating – it keeps the character of the piece.

The point here is that there are degrees of restoration. There are restorers who are sympathetic geniuses and there are restorers who are mass murderers, the Charles Mansens of the antiques trade. I would give £1,000 to some restorers not to go near my piece under any circumstances, because they are given a wonderful, antique piece and promptly destroy it. If you spend £5,000 on a piece of furniture and take it to the wrong man, you'll wind up with £2,000-worth of furniture. Unsympathetic, uncaring restoration is out-and-out wholesale slaughter. I know a shop out in the country where the dealer only buys cheap, cheerful furniture, tables and chairs for say, the German market. His restorers come in and they've got mechanical sanders! They sand off the whole surface, then it's on with the red splosh, same colour all over. On with the French polish until it comes up like a skating rink. When they've finished, that piece has been completely destroyed. It has no character, no feel about it any more. To me it's horrifying, but there is a market for these pieces.

Nevertheless, generally I find that my clients prefer sympathetically restored pieces, as I do. Collectors of French 18th-century furniture want it in the condition it was in 1780, when the colours of the woods were bright and vivid, and the gilding was absolutely spot on. Dutch marquetry is similar, also made of coloured woods. When the craftsmen were making it, they used to put the veneers into hot sand, which produced a rich array of hues and shades. This technique was ideal for making those wonderful flowers, like peonies and tulips, that you see on Dutch furniture. The effect is extraordinarily hard to reproduce during restoration though, which is why you can spot a restored piece a mile away; modern craftsmen unfortunately just don't have the same skills.

When I get a piece of French or Dutch furniture, my restorer uses a paste – rather like a T-cutting process on a car – to cut back the surface of old wax which has attracted dirt and grime over the years and built up in numerous thick layers to give a distorted, dirty colour. He doesn't go through the French polish to the bare wood because he doesn't want to have to repolish it. Then he applies wax, layer upon layer, to get a rich colour. He adopts a similar approach with ancient layers of beeswax. He does not cut back right through 200 years of wax to get to a bare wood, because if he did all the patina, the character, would go. The English have a much more subtle taste in antiques than other nationalities. They appreciate the fading of 200 years of sunlight on a piece of walnut. And to my mind restoration should be subtle, too. You have to understand antiques and love them to know how far you can go, and to recognize when a restorer has gone too far. If you want to get seriously into buying and collecting antiques, do what I did – hunt around for a sympathetic restorer. You'll never regret it, even if he charges a little more for his services.

Restoring fabrics

Everything I have said so far about restoration does not necessarily refer to chairs, sofas, settees and chaise longues. Wood does not wear out easily, and when it does, that worn edge can lend it value because it shows its age. But fabrics have only a very limited life. It stands to reason, because of fabric's constant use, that it's going to become threadbare and shabby. Springs will poke through, you will see the horsehair stuffing, and there may be ugly spills and stains – all spoiling the look of a piece in your beautiful room.

The style of a chair or sofa is dependent on its framework, which you will want to preserve and bring back to its best; but the actual fabric can be stripped right back to its innards and replaced without losing all its value. In fact, if you choose a good upholsterer and spend time on choosing good-quality fabric that is sympathetic in period to the piece, you will be enhancing its value.

There are times, however, when removing covering is not always advisable if it can be avoided. Say you have a set of chairs that have 18th-century needlepoint covering. Of course you will want to keep the covering, up to a reasonable point. If they're worn and a little bit shabby I would suggest taking the covers off carefully and sending them to a school of needlework to have them restored and repaired. But it could be that they are so shabby that they're no longer usable except in a museum setting. They will be fine there as examples of wonderful chairs with original tapestry on them, which will be admired behind glass cases in a moth-free, child-free zone, but you couldn't use them in your home.

If you are fortunate enough to own such a set of chairs, you'd use your common sense to decide whether to have the original covering restored or get a new covering. Choose whichever option is the most practical. If you decide on new covering, you could always save the original covers in case you want to sell your chairs. Or you could clean and frame them: such things make interesting decorative talking points hanging on your wall.

Now, if you're talking about something much more valuable, such as a set of highly valuable Queen Anne chairs worth £40,000 or £60,000, with frayed but original covers on them, there's no question that the covering is all part of the value and removing it would not be advisable in any circumstances. If there comes a time when these are no longer suitable as chairs for sitting on or dining on; they should be preserved as objects, not usable furniture.

6

Recycling

Many people seem to have an idea that once you have bought an antique there is some kind of sacred mystique about it and it's yours for life; but it doesn't have to be. It should be yours for as long as you get pleasure from it or have a use for it. Call it the dealer in me, but I love the idea of recycling antiques. There is something so sensible and organic about it that I would recommend it every time.

Why sell?

Over the years my taste in antiques has definitely changed. I won't say for the better, because everything has its beauty and value and appeal, and anything is 'good' and worth collecting or owning if it personally appeals to you and is the best example you can find. It's just changed, as, I think, everybody's taste changes to some extent, both as they grow older and as they learn more.

When I was young, things like copper jam pans fascinated me. In our technological age, we sometimes forget that ordinary people had to make most things at home and there have been some pretty peculiar contraptions made to stuff sausages, core apples, sharpen knives or fill oil lamps or, indeed, to serve some obscure purpose for which there is absolutely no use today. Things that had a sense of nostalgia or history about them appealed to me. I loved the stories behind everyday, useful pieces and was avidly curious about strange and unusual bits of brass. What were they? What were they used for? Where did they come from? Who lived with them?

I wanted to find as much as I could about the men and women who used these objects and about those who made them out of raw materials, with few tools. From looking at the craftsmanship in the smaller, useful pieces that I could afford and put on display or hang on my wall (such as a brass bed warmer or a chaffing dish) I started to perceive the craftsmanship in furniture, which ultimately became my speciality. With my interest in finer furniture came the desire to have more refined and elegant objects, such as prints and oil paintings and a handsome mirror or two hanging on my walls. The copper and brass bits and pieces didn't fit in any longer and I decided to sell, or recycle, them, which is partly how I got into dealing.

So in this way my career in antiques didn't originate with buying things as an investment and having their resale value in mind; but my changing taste made an understanding of value a side-effect of my original purchases. When I came to sell things I no longer wanted, I saw for myself first-hand what had kept its value, what had lost its value and what had increased in value. It's when you sell that you see how good your buying really is. If you want to compete with the professionals in the saleroom you have to learn, just as they did. Remember, a professional was a beginner once. If you put goods that you have bought back into the market-place and lose money, it teaches us to be a lot more careful next time.

You might have bought a little writing desk, and really enjoyed it, but there may come a time when you want a larger desk, or you move and there is no room for that desk. That's where recycling comes in. Or you could have inherited something you're not keen on. You decide to sell and use that money to buy something else. Another reason to sell is perhaps when you have bought a single nice object that takes your fancy – an antique quilt or a lacquer box to use as an ornament; you then spot another and buy that, and before you know it, you've become a collector and all available space is overflowing. At that point you may well decide to have a clear-out to get rid of some of the excess pieces, or to use the money to buy better-quality pieces.

Trading up

Many collectors sell poor-quality objects when they see better ones because it is the ultimate aim of a collector to own the very best in their chosen subject. Take the bisque piano babies I talked about on page 109. You might have bought a seaside baby (that's the adorable little girl with the bucket and spade) and her bucket is either missing or replaced. If you see a perfect one, with everything original, of course you will want that one instead; and the logical thing to do would be to sell the one you already have for the highest price you can get in order to help finance your new baby. Or perhaps, when it was just the two of you, you bought a small dining table, but now your family has grown and with guests you regularly need to seat up to fourteen. Nobody wants two dining tables, do they? So you sell the small table and buy a larger one.

When I was younger I bought a brass lamp. Twelve months later I decided that it was a little over the top so I sold it and bought a Spode one because of its finer points and style. We all have examples in our everyday lives of deciding we don't like something any more; but the difference is that if you buy almost anything new, whether it is furniture, books, carpets, a car or clothes, as soon as you buy it, it's depreciated in value, as you quickly discover when you come to sell. In fact, with some things like clothes and books there is no point in selling them for a few pence. It's far better just to give them away to a charity shop. You would never dream of giving antiques away. You can always sell them and often at a profit, and trade up to something you like.

S e l l i n g   o n

The most obvious place to sell would be through a card in a local shop window or an advertisement in a local paper – and here we have come full cycle from Chapter Four. You will never get very much from a card in the window. My advice to you would be that if you bought the piece in an antiques shop, return there either to sell it back or trade it for something you would like to own.

There are many dealers you can go to and say, 'Look, I like the kind of things that you buy and sell. I'm going to be a regular shopper with you, but from time to time I may change my mind. I might want to bring something back. What would be your position on that?' The dealer's first instinct might be to shake his head, but you can get into dialogue. Tell him that if you bring something back, you don't necessarily want money for it. You could trade up or put whatever price you agree on towards something else. Point out to him that he'll make a profit; after all, it would be naïve to think that he will give you exactly what you paid for it. I can almost guarantee that he will listen to you, as I can almost guarantee that you will get considerably more for whatever it is you are recycling than if it were a modern object.

Things
I Wish
I'd Never
Sold

Now that I've explained the principles and given you some tips, let me broaden out the picture — and, I hope, whet your appetite — by showing you and passing on my experience of some of the most outstanding antiques that I've come across.

Some of the Best

When I buy an object, it's mine until I sell it. I try not to get too attached however, because I am a dealer, in the business of buying and selling beautiful things. The problem is when you have a limited capital you must buy the goods and sell them, make a profit, pay your salary and expenses and repeat the exercise. But because I am constantly excited by each new object as it comes my way, and I never buy things which I personally don't like because I cannot sell something that I don't believe in, now and then I feel in my heart a lingering affection for those special pieces I no longer have.

I've bought a few superb objects over the past 25 years that I have let go with regret, pain almost, and I have spent the intervening years trying to buy one or two of them back! Here are a few of my favourite things.

My first great buy

When I first started in business, round about 1976, within the first twelve months I made my first major purchase: a rare olive wood cabinet (see right). It was probably made by Gillows, though I didn't realize it at the time, decorated with Wedgwood plaques. Originally it was ordered by a Sheffield steel magnate as part of a suite of furniture of several pieces to furnish a wing in his home when the Prince of Wales (later Edward V11) and the Princess of Wales came to visit him. When I bought it from an antiques dealer in Sheffield I thought I had paid the earth for it – I paid about £6,000 – so I was over the moon when I sold it a private client for about £7,500. I thought I had swum the Channel under water without an aqualung! It was only later that I got pangs of bereavement over it, since when I've been trying to buy it back.

I have rung the owner and said: 'You know that wonderful large cabinet I sold you? Have you ever thought about selling it? I'm prepared to give you enough for you to make a very handsome profit.' But his regular response is: 'It looks nice where it is. I think I'll keep it.' He's not even interested in a considerable profit. If I bought it back I would never sell it.

Long-case (or grandfather) clocks

In my earlier days I'd go to a sale at a very early hour in the morning, view and stay there all day, listening to tales from old antiques dealers – wonderful tales of amazing pieces of furniture which don't readily turn up today, but which were plentiful in England in the 1920s and 1930s, before millions of pounds' worth was shipped away.

These old timers would reminisce over pieces they had bought and sold, but their favourite pieces were nearly always long-case clocks. They'd say things like, 'You never really own a long-case clock; it stays with you for only your portion of life then goes on long after you have gone. Family after family, generation after generation, live their short span with that clock. It's almost like a living thing ticking away, the heart of a home. When you're alone in a room with a grandfather clock, you sit back with your glass of wine, your pint of wallop, and feel at ease with the world at the end of a hard day.'

For some reason these clocks

were out of fashion for a time and dealers would have dozens of them lined up in their premises; you could take your pick at about £25 a time. I went through a stage when I first started collecting when I must had twenty clocks in the house, all ticking and chiming away until eventually Lorne said, 'Enough is enough.'

One I wish I had kept was a fine example of a late 17th-century marquetry clock, signed John Finch, London. The case was elaborately decorated with chains of leaves, flowers and exotic birds. It had everything, elegance, style and beauty. It was feminine and masculine at the same time without being over the top. Some of these fine clocks have been butchered over the years, usually with the bases being cut down to fit smaller rooms. But this one was in wonderful original condition. I sold it in 1979 for about £5,000; today it would probably sell for up to £25,000.

Act of Parliament clocks

Another clock I should never have sold was by Wicksteed of Wolverhampton, dated approximately 1790. These mural, or wall, clocks, are nearly always fitted with pendulums; the waisted long trunk cases are usually lacquered in gold or black or dark green background; some have painted decoration or scenes; and they have large octagonal or circular faces with no covering glass. Their name is historical and interesting. In 1797, William Pitt's government imposed a tax of five shillings a year on all clocks, whether used in a private home or a public place. Such a tax was enormously unpopular; not only did it bring the clockmaking industry to the verge of bankruptcy, and many thousands of clocks and watches were destroyed by owners who could not pay the tax, but people found it hard to go about their daily lives on time. The tax was repealed after a year, but meanwhile innkeepers all over the country adopted an already existing style of clock, possibly because of the large size of the face, to hang in their public rooms for the benefit of their customers. These clocks became known as Act of Parliament tavern clocks and come on the market from time to time.

Following the principle of always buying the best that your pocket can afford, I paid I think about £9,000 for it, which was a lot of money then for an Act of Parliament clock, but it was worth it as this one was exceptional. Apart from the fact that it was a striker (normally they are only time pieces) most importantly, and this point applies to all antiques, the original paintwork and gilding was all there, even down to the wonderful little oil painting in the door. If I live to be 100 I will never find a better example of a tavern clock than this. It amazed me that it survived 200 years of wear and tear in such perfect condition. I let it go for £12,000. Today (five years later) it would probably be worth £18,000. There are many tavern clocks still to be found at £7,000–£9,000, but none like this beauty.

Another one I wish I had never sold is a *standing* tavern clock. Nobody I know in the business has ever seen anything like it since. I should never have parted with this one, either. It has an inscription to Jacob Hill and a Latin inscription which refers to the eating club in which it stood. It means something like 'Good life and good times', which we would all wish for.

A pietra dura table

This type of table (top right) would have been bought in Italy by a young gentleman on his grand tour of Europe, a kind of educational coming out that wealthy young men undertook almost up to the outbreak of the First World War. The one I bought was dated *circa* 1860–70, 1.5m (5ft) across with a lavishly decorated floral top of assorted coloured marbles inlaid on a slate bed on a giltwood stand. Both top and stand were Italian. The gilding needed reburnishing and the slate a little restoration work, but otherwise the table was in pristine condition.

Often the tops only of these tables were transported home and a base would be specially made here, as in the case of another example (bottom right) which, to me, is a far finer specimen. The top was Italian and the wonderfully carved Regency pedestal base of rosewood was made *circa* 1830 by William Trotter, a fine Edinburgh furniture maker. The detail and workmanship of both top and base was superb (in the photograph the base looks like two kinds of wood, but it is just the way the light hits it). I like the history of these pieces, the idea of wealthy young men collecting these fine things during a time when travelling was far more exotic than it is today.

The maharaja's davenport 1839

As far as we know, the first recorded Davenport was made in the late 18th century (perhaps 1790–1800). The first one we know about was recorded in Gillows' archives as a small desk made for a Captain Davenport. Military men took these pieces in a carrying box on tours of duty, not as a lighter campaign piece to be set up in their tents on the battlefield with them, but to use in their own homes.

I have owned several Davenports, including a magnificent Gillows one (page 136) and one (opposite) belonging to the Maharaja of Visakapatnam, which was possibly the most spectacular and rarest example ever made. It was ivory veneered over a sandalwood carcass etched with black penwork, a kind of black resin that would have been rubbed in the etching to make the overall decoration depicting Hindu gods, Ganesh, Krishna and so on. It had lions' paw feet, indicating its fitness for a mogul, silver fittings, handles, locks and hinges; drawers with wonderful fretted ivory work veneered to the surface; and a chessboard top of tortoise or turtleshell and ivory squares. The chess set that went with it was of buffalo horn, typical of the region where this type of work went on (you often find smaller objects, such as writing boxes and tea caddies in this style). What is interesting to me is the thought that a serving officer must have been in India in the days of the Raj with a Davenport – perhaps even one by Gillows – which the Maharaja obviously saw and admired and had his palace workmen produce one for him with this very Anglo-Indian feel.

This Davenport had gone to Christie's (where I bought it) from the estate of an elderly person in Bath who had had a huge collection of antiques, all in a terrible state after years of neglect. A lot of the Davenport's ivory was loose or missing and had to be reglued or replaced. Inside one of the drawers I found a small card written by hand: 'Exhibited by the Maharaja of Visakapatnam. Executed by the palace workmen.' I couldn't figure out what this meant and decided to research further. I got copies of the *Indian Gazette* and I traced the particular maharaja mentioned to about the 1880s. I knew that the Davenport was made before then, so it struck me that the piece must have been made for his father.

I showed the piece at an international fair and a specialist chess dealer came along. He thought the Davenport was fabulous and the following day he rang me. 'I've just remembered something,' he said. 'I think I've read about this.' He said that the maharajah on the card came to London in the 1880s–90s as a sponsor of the world chess championship, in association with one of Queen Victoria's sons. I imagine the maharaja must have brought this little chess Davenport with him, and in a complete reversal of the usual pattern of these campaign pieces going off to the other side of the world with the British, exhibited it in London. I found out that this particular maharaja was a favourite of Queen Victoria, who loved all her maharajas. I had solved the mystery of the exhibition – there was so much history wrapped up in this one fascinating and beautiful object.

Much as I loved it, as a hardworking dealer with little capital, I couldn't keep it. With restoration it cost me about £20,000 and eventually I sold it

a year later for a very small 10 per cent margin. I believe it now resides in a famous London shop, on sale for a fabulous sum.

A late Regency Davenport by Gillows (page 136), dated approximately 1790, was another of the nicest I have owned. It had drawers to one side and dummies to the other, and was English through and through, with a wonderful colour. The figuring on the walnut was absolutely amazing, the veneers perfectly matched in

every way. It would have been taken to somewhere in the Empire by a serving officer. A third one (right) was Oriental, made in Canton in China, where there was a thriving industry in manufacturing goods for the European market. All the drawers had Chinese character marks on them. It was made of amboyna (also known as padauk) wood, with ivory stringing, wonderful recessed brass military-style handles, nice solid carrying handles and an original silk velvet writing slope. The brass candlesticks would have been taken off and stored in a drawer when the piece was transported.

If I had had the money and the space, I would have kept all three of these exceptional pieces of furniture.

Bust of a young woman

This exquisite piece was by the famous Italian sculptor, Pietro Calvi (1833–1884), and the quality just shone out. Apart from the fact that I would have loved to have kept her, I am including it here to illustrate a restoration point. When I found her she was filthy dirty. It is not easy to clean marble. Chemicals are used and an over-enthusiastic application of them can take off the 'skin', that almost gleaming radiant patina that the finest marble pieces have. Never attempt to clean marble yourself. Indeed, if any piece of art needs cleaning always consult an expert.(This reminds me of something I saw recently – incredibly, someone had *sand-blasted* a bronze group back to the almost raw yellow look that is there before the artist applies the traditional greeny-brown patina that more usually comes with great age. Its value was instantly reduced by two-thirds, and it looked absolutely terrible.)

The Minstrel

At the top of my list of things I wish I had never parted with is a statue of a minstrel, in combined media of bronze and assorted marbles. His waistcoat, shirt and scarf were in different coloured marbles, made in pieces and somehow cleverly put together; the face and hands were bronze, the hat plaster and the banjo slate. It was also by Pietro Calvi. In my research I found out that Calvi exhibited many pieces, including *The Minstrel*, at the Royal Academy in London and the Salon of Paris. One of his most well-known pieces is a bust of Othello, or the Moor of Venice (below), again in combined media of white marble and bronze. I've seen the Othello and it always struck me that there was a strong resemblance

between the Negro figure and *The Minstrel*. I found that in the mid-19th century a black American actor, Ira Aldridge,

came to Europe and played Othello, the first black man to play him on stage, at Drury Lane, going on to tour Europe to massive critical acclaim. Apart from classical roles he also played light musical and comedy roles. This made me feel sure that Aldridge had also sat for *The Minstrel*. The possibility was also supported by

the fact that there were Negro minstrels coming to Europe and doing black minstrel shows in the 1830s at places like Vauxhall Gardens in London. There have also been many lesser-quality spelter (base metal) minstrels made that reflect this influx, usually entitled 'Bojangles' – I have even sold a similar one, entitled 'Oh What a Fly!' (left) an attractive and amusing bronzed figure of a minstrel boy playing a banjo, smiling because a fly had settled on his nose, but these, while having a charm of their own, should never be confused with Calvi's work. He is a master and his work is of a very high, exhibition quality.

I took *The Minstrel* to the fair at Olympia and showed it with a price tag of around £30,000. A pleasant young American lady came to my stand, casually dressed in a zip-up trainer suit and sneakers and with three or four young children. *The Minstrel* caught her attention and we spoke about it for about half an hour. I did not think this woman was a potential purchaser – I thought perhaps she was a tourist – but as always I was happy to speak to anybody, whether a cleaning lady or someone wearing a 10-carat diamond ring, who came along to see the goods I was exhibiting, and obviously I talked about them in the most glowing terms because I only buy what I like, and I just love this figure. After asking the price she said, 'I'll send my husband along.' I didn't pay too much attention because that is a common 'get-out' line. Next day a man came up to the stand. As soon as he walked on, I felt there was something quite imposing about this tall chunky guy in a designer shirt and a long pigtail. He was Phil Collins' manager. He told me his wife had sent him along to buy *The Minstrel* for the Elizabethan minstrel's gallery in their rambling home in the English countryside, and I am delighted to say that is where he ended up, a perfect little spot for him.

To show you the kind of work a dealer puts in on almost every piece, I will mention that before exhibiting *The Minstrel* I first offered it to Oprah Winfrey, who is a very big collector of art. This is her letter declining (below). I would later say to her, 'You missed out on this, Oprah – the figure is now worth at least £100,000!'

HARPO PRODUCTIONS, INC.
110 North Carpenter Street
Chicago, Illinois 60607
312.633.1000   Fax 312.633.1111

Oprah Winfrey
Chairman of the Board

HARPO

Producers of
The Oprah Winfrey Show
Primetime Oprah

January 25, 1991

Mr. David H. Dickinson
David H. Dickinson Ltd.
17/19 John Dalton Street
Manchester M2 6FW
ENGLAND

Dear Mr. Dickinson,

Thank you for giving me time to consider purchasing the bust of Pietro Calvi, however, I am not interested in such a purchase at this time. Therefore, I am returning the photos to you.

The Best,

Oprah Winfrey

Oprah Winfrey

OW:ah
Enclosure

The boudoir grand

In my shop in Manchester I had a magnificent John Broadwood inlaid boudoir grand piano (not full size). I allowed a tough entrepreneurial property dealer to twist my arm, and after two week's haggling, like a fool I eventually succumbed to his persuasion and sold it to him for £11,000. I think I made £2,000 profit. Barely five years later it came up in a London sale and from memory I think it made about £35,000. We go back to the same old thing – when you see something fabulous, don't be afraid to pay the asking price. Had the entrepreneur failed to buy the piano by trying to be too sharp, he would have missed out on a wonderful item and an eventual high profit.

The painted screen

I saw a six-panel folding painted leather screen at a house sale conducted by a firm called Henry Spencer (see page 105) at Bagshaw Hall outside Nottingham. It was catalogued as late 19th-century Dutch, in the manner of Melchior D'Hondercoeter, a 17th-century Dutch painter who specialized in bird studies. The great thing about this was it had all the decorative attributes that people are looking for today: an abundance of domestic and wild fowl and other fantastical birds, lyrical garlands and a gorgeous landscape. It was an amazing thing in wonderful condition.

At the sale it was estimated at £3,000–£4,000 but everyone bid for it and I took it to £11,000 in the teeth of fierce competition. After some minor restoration I sold it for about £16,000. But I made a bad mistake – it was worth about £40,000–£50,000. I sold it to a very astute collector, the same man who bought the Mandarin figure (see page 78), who did some research where I'd missed out. Bagshaw Hall had been a royal residence at one time (I think it was where the Quorn Hunt used to start from) and he found that the screen had been in the inventory of the house for about 250 years. It was therefore actually early 18th century.

The Ebo cabinet

This was a spectacular 19th-century Japanese Ebo cabinet, lacquered in black and gold. It was originally made to stand on the floor, but I had a modern plain black lacquer stand made for it with an Oriental feel in keeping with contemporary decorating trends. I loved it so much that I dearly wanted to keep it but I couldn't afford to. I sold it for about £30,000 to an American who has a home in this country.

The Japanese cockatoo

The photograph does not do this justice. The 19th-century bird, made from solid ivory, standing on a gnarled tree root, was absolutely lifelike.
It appeared to have the actual texture that occurs when a bird shakes itself and ruffles its feathers and they float down; the feathers seem to be in motion. This wonderful object is now worth about £10,000. I don't know why I didn't keep it.

The little admiral

This was one of my all-time favourite pieces, partly because I fell in love with it, and partly because it involves part of my history in the business and reminds me of where I was.

Twenty-five years ago, whenever my partner Chris Haworth and I came down to the big London sales we'd stand at night on the pavements, staring into our favourite London galleries, looking at the shops lit up, getting ideas and getting excited. We were so young and enthusiastic that we couldn't wait to start putting some of our ideas into practice (this was where we got the idea of putting the big Sèvres vases in the window on their own as a focal point – see page 36).

There was one shop in particular in fashionable Jermyn Street that I admired, and that fired me towards unusual objects. The owner, Arthur Davidson, is retired now but many people who read this book and go back a few years might remember him. His shop had the most extraordinarily eclectic collection, from huge telescopes to 15th-century tables. One night I saw a little carved figure of an admiral holding a sextant that had stood over the doorway of Frodsham's, a famous nautical and naval technical equipment suppliers. Nelson had walked though that doorway and bought his sextant, his telescopes and, for all I know, a chronometer. One night some young high-spirited naval cadets thought the little admiral must be missing the sea. As a prank, they stole him and whisked him off to Portsmouth aboard their ship. He sailed around the world, experiencing adventures and storms. A year later he was mysteriously restored to his position above the shop, and I like to think he settled back happily to life as a landlubber with his memories. Two hundred years passed; Frodsham's closed down and Arthur Davidson bought the little admiral.

Somehow that story fired my imagination and all the romance in me. I was smitten and went back time and time again to stare into the brightly lit interior, gazing at the quaint little wooden figure. He was in the shop for quite a long time, so one day I summoned up courage and went in to confront Mr Davidson, a very slick businessman with a cashmere sweater who always had a large cigar in his hand.

'Excuse me, Mr Davidson, how much is that carved figure?'

He looked me up and down, took a few puffs as if to say, 'Who is this? Does he look as if he's got any money?' Finally, in his deep voice he said, '£3,800.' A bit superior was Arthur Davidson, married to Lesley Grade's daughter, Linda. (A story had gone the rounds, originating I think from Linda. Old Mrs Grade, Sir Lew and Lesley's mother, was at one of these royal variety performances when Sir Bernard Delfont, also her son, introduced her to the Queen Mother: 'Your Majesty, may I introduce you to my mother?' The Queen Mum said: 'How nice to meet you. You must be very proud of your children.' And old Mrs Grade, in her very thick middle European accent, said, 'And you of yours.')

Back to the little admiral. We'd only been in business for about 18 months and didn't have that kind of money – and Arthur Davidson knew it. But about a year later the little admiral was still there. By now I was getting a bit more confident, and had a bit more money, so again I went in and said, 'Mr Davidson, you probably won't remember me, but some time ago I wanted to buy the little figure. I notice you haven't sold it and, if it's not being rude, would you take a bid from me?'

Arthur Davidson looked at me over the smoke curling from his big cigar and said slowly, 'Well, if you're not too silly about it.'

I said, 'I'll give you £2,500 for it now.'

He looked at me, drew consideringly on his cigar and said. 'Make it £2,800 and you've bought it.'

I said, 'Right!' fast, slapped hands and it was done.

I had bought something from someone who at this stage I felt was my hero in the business. 'I'm in now!" I thought to myself.

I made the cheque out, and Arthur Davidson said, 'I'll have to clear it you know.'

'That's all right, Mr Davidson. It will clear – and when it does, I'll arrange transport for the figure.' From never daring to step foot in this establishment, I was now as bold as brass and dashed around the shop asking the price of practically everything in it. I could see him puffing the cigar and thinking, 'Little upstart, is he going to buy anything else?' My welcome was starting to

wear a bit thin. I walked into the window where there was a huge 16th-century Armada chest, a fabulous thing, and asked, 'And how much is that?'

Arthur Davidson puffed on his cigar and said, '*That* is a lot of money.' I knew then it was time to go.

From our little shop in Disley, the Old Bellows, Chris and I advertised the little admiral on the back page of *Art and Antiques Weekly*, which was quite audacious for newcomers in the trade since the magazine was highly respected and went out to all the top collectors and dealers everywhere. But we had some big ideas and were buying some fabulous things even in 1978. The advertisement read: 'An important and rare 18th-century wooden figure of a little admiral holding a brass sextant. The figure was formerly mounted above the premises of Charles Frodsham and Co. Ltd., and is probably one of few such figures remaining outside museum collections. Height 5ft.'

After being in this wonderful shop in the heart of St James's for a year and not selling, back in our little village in Cheshire, it sold as soon as it was advertised. Within three days

the phone rang. It was a call from a man in Malvern, Worcestershire, who was interested in nautical figures. He came up and bought the little admiral for £3,800. Jubilant though I was at making a sale, I almost wept. From the moment he left the shop, I wanted my little figure back. Since 1978 I have rung this man several times and said to him, 'Put what price you want to on him, I'll pay it.' To me it's priceless. But he won't sell at any price, and I can't say I blame him.

Collinson
and Lock

The firm of Collinson and Lock
could be called the forgotten
geniuses. They were a
fashionable and high-class West
End company whose
enterprising activities from
1870 to 1897 making the most
exquisite, ornate and elegant
furniture tell a typical Victorian
story of commercial success.
When Frank Collinson and
George Lock joined forces to
produce 'artistic' furniture they
succeeded beyond their wildest
expectations, causing a sensation
at the many exhibitions at
which they showed. I admire
their furniture because it is
daring and beautiful, at the
cutting edge of its day and still
stunning today. It's now being
recognized for the sheer quality
and artistry that went into its
manufacture and many
Collinson and Lock pieces are in
the Victoria and Albert
Museum. Amazingly enough,
until fairly recently, nobody
collected Collinson and Lock
and the most wonderful pieces
could be snapped up for
buttons. I wish I could say the
same today.

I bought as many of these
pieces as I could while they were

still relatively affordable, including some (opposite and below) that were rosewood and ivory inlaid Renaissance revival style, designed by Stephen Webb, who joined the firm as chief designer-craftsman, after training at the South Kensington School of Art. After the firm was wound up he went on to be head of sculpture at the Royal College of Art. Prices are going up fast and furiously.

That's why I say on many occasions in this book: *look for what appeals to your eye and buy quality*. Many of the highest-quality makers of the 19th century did the most superb work and as we now approach the 21st century these pieces are taking on a whole different meaning and value.

Late 18th-century Chinese Export lacquered bureau bookcase of small delicate proportions

Shown here are the exterior and interior of a delightful piece, of small and delicate proportions, that I sold to a dear friend and a most amazing lady, for her apartment in Belgravia. I have included them because that sale was the start of a long personal friendship. She is 87 years of age, spends half her time in her beautiful home in Jamaica, where she entertains lavishly (Lorne and I have just come back from spending Christmas with her). The most wonderful person, her energy and enthusiasm for life leaves me flagging – in fact, I nearly decided to run off with her. I also love the piece I sold her and would have liked to have kept it myself. I have to keep reminding myself that I am a dealer and not a collector.

Display cabinet, 1936

This display cabinet in satinwood is part of a large suite which includes an exotic cocktail cabinet, a three-piece bérgère suite, a pair of standard lamps, a table and a mirror with chinoiserie panels. I have included it here because, apart from the fact that I wish I had kept it, it is an example of how something doesn't have to be an antique to be collectable or for quality to shine out. Strictly speaking it is not an antique, being less than 100 years old. However, it is the most wonderful exhibition-quality, Chippendale-style, chinoiserie decorated piece, made in 1936 by Hillie and Co. When I exhibited at Olympia in 1981, Rudolf Nureyev was brought to see it by his interior decorator and was considering it for his apartment in New York; but before he made up his mind, I sold it to an old mate of mine, Peter Stringfellow, for his offices in what was then the new Hippodrome. God knows what kind of sights this suite has seen or how many ladies have sat on those bérgère cushions. Always a game one, Peter!

Paintings

If you are buying a painting as an investment as much as a decorative item to hang on your wall, choose the subject with care. Some of the following examples might show you why I say this. It is not always easy to anticipate what might later prove hard to sell, because art is very much a matter of personal taste. As a dealer who doesn't buy and sell that many pictures, I have a slight lack of experience in choosing subjects, of knowing what is going to be popular and what is going to prove more difficult in the market-place. I have found that sometimes it is just a matter of persevering until the right buyer comes along. But at the end of the day you have to rely on your taste and buy what you enjoy looking at.

Because I don't buy many pictures as a rule, I go in for quality with interesting furnishing or decorative value to them. There are so many specialist art dealers out there with a wide circle of clients, so I look for something different even in the picture market-place. The following stories reflect how some paintings practically sell themselves, while with others, you have to work that bit harder to find the right buyer.

Pollak, Woman with dove, 1852

This is a very fashionable subject and the price reflected that. Orientalist subjects over the past 20 years have really caught on and this was no exception. The subject is a lady in an Orientalist costume with a turban. The charming thing about it is that she is releasing a dove, which is perhaps carrying a *billet doux* or a love letter, so it has a romantic feel to it. It was a huge picture, about 2.5m (8 ft) by 1.25m (4 ft). I showed it at Olympia and almost immediately, a lady came along who fell in love with it. She said she would buy it if it would fit a particular space on her wall. Well, sometimes when people say that, you never see them again; but this lady went home and measured, returned and bought it. Today, as you come into the door of her apartment, you see the picture hanging on the wall at the end of the long corridor facing you. It just fits the space with an inch to spare and looks wonderful. I see the owner a couple of times a year at the fairs and I always say, 'How's our girl?'

Laura Knight,
Boy in the chair

I took a loss with a large oil painting by Laura Knight of a young boy in a chair because I hadn't taken into account the fact that it can be quite hard to sell modern portraits, no matter how charming the subject. Dame Laura and her husband used to stay at a house in Devon where a circle of artists once gathered. The owner of the property was an artist, and his young son became the subject of this painting, seated in a nice little period child's chair. When I first saw the picture I thought, 'This is a real winner, a mischievous little boy, with scuffed toes on his sandals.' But, despite trying hard, for some reason I did not find a home for this even though it was a large picture, wonderfully well painted in oils and signedj154 . The price I bought it for from a dealer friend, £5,500, should have warned me that there might have been a slight problem. If this had been one of Laura Knight's circus pictures, the price range would have been at least £25,000–£30,000. At first I thought my lack of success in finding a buyer was because portraits are notoriously difficult to sell. This is not so much the case with period portraits, because they can be put on to your wall in a period house where they lend character, but contemporary subjects, even if by a famous artist, usually have to mean something to the buyer. I showed this at Olympia and the only real interest was from a lady who came on to the stand one day and said, 'I know who that is. I was engaged to him. Now he's an artist in Australia.'

I realized from comments that the picture's unpopularity had nothing to do with the lack of quality; it was the subject. A lot of people seemed uncomfortable with the combination of a little boy and a large riding crop. But I think it was purely chance that they had sat him in that chair and had found that particular prop to hold (riding stuff and so on would naturally be lying about in a large country house). Eventually, I traded it back to the dealer chum of mine whom I bought it from, taking a loss of about £1,500. It just shows you that in paintings, subject matter is important.

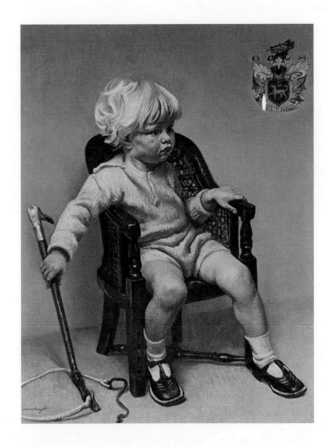

Girardet, The Siege of Zaragossa, *1879*

I've always just followed my gut instinct when it comes to buying and this was no exception. It was to my eyes an amazing picture, depicting the final hours of the siege of Zaragossa when Napoleon's troops invaded Spain. When I bought this at a major London saleroom (from memory for about £9,000) the sheer quality of this picture in relationship to the area of canvas made it seem to me very inexpensive, but the consensus of dealers within the art trade was that it was very uncommercial because of its huge size, 3.5m (9ft) by 1.25m (4ft), and subject matter: a spectacular battle scene raging with Napoleonic soldiers fighting with resistance fighters including the legendary Maid of Zaragossa and even a priest wielding a crucifix during a particularly vicious siege where a lot of blood was spilled. My dealer chums informed me that people did not like to see blood in the pictures they bought for their home.

I admired both the quality of the work and the dramatic subject, the size, and I thought it would sell easily to some company chairman for his large boardroom, its size being more suited to a museum or a salon (it had been exhibited at the Salon of Paris). When I showed it at Olympia people admired it but they didn't buy it. Shortly afterwards, Lorne and I went on holiday to Malaysia and on the flight sat next to a young lady, and as the ten-hour journey progressed we got into conversation. We learned that she was a nanny going to Hong Kong, where her employer was the president of a Spanish bank, and, amazingly, he was the present Duke of Zaragossa. I undid my briefcase in which I had a copy of the picture, handed it to her and asked if she would pass it on to her employer. About two months later I received a charming letter from him saying that he admired the picture but he did not have space to accommodate it. He had passed the photograph on to the president of another Spanish bank.

A year later, three weeks before I was due to show at Olympia again, I got a letter from the president of this other bank telling me that his bank was considering a corporate purchase of this item for its boardroom. I wrote back and said I didn't want to appear to be putting any pressure on him but since I was shortly exhibiting the painting, his board would have to make a decision very quickly. On the opening day of the fair a young Iranian came on to the stand, looked at the picture for a long time, went away and came back with his wife. She liked it, and he said he would go into his office in the city on the following day, a Saturday, measure up, and if the painting fitted he would buy it. I agreed to reserve it for him and we negotiated a price, about £15,000 (not a great deal of profit for something I had held

for about 18 months.) Within about five minutes of him leaving the stand a Spanish businessman, nothing to do with the Spanish bank, walked on and stared hard at the painting and decided to buy it for a new commercial building he owned in Zaragossa. He said, 'I would be taking it back to where it belongs.'

On being informed that I had promised that I would reserve this picture until 12 o'clock the following day at a price of £15,000, the Spaniard offered £16,000. When you give your word to somebody, when you involve yourself in a contract, a shake of hands is as binding as a written contract. I said, 'Look, I'd love to sell you the picture, but I have given someone else my word that I will reserve it for him until 12 o'clock tomorrow.'

I had a bit of a wander around the fair, found the Iranian and explained that I was not on a mission to pressurize him, but he had to be sure to stick to our deadline. The following morning he came in at ten o'clock promptly with a cheque. Unfortunately the Spaniard telephoned me at five past twelve and I had to disappoint him. I could have got more money from him, but that's not business. News travels fast in the antiques world and if you are a bit devious your reputation suffers.

Decorative Pieces

I have sold many objects that were made for one purpose or another, but today are bought solely as decoration for the home. Some of these items might be obvious, such as a copper kettle, but other objects on a larger scale are also used as sculptural items to make a dramatic statement.

Telescopes

Both these Victorian telescopes are serious, professional pieces of equipment, usable today. And so handsome, with such line and style and purpose that even if you don't know a star from a planet, you could put them in your home as a strong focus and talking point for a room or a conservatory. Often these are bought for the reception areas or boardrooms of corporate buildings. Or I can imagine such objects going into some wonderful sea front apartment in Malibu or Hong Kong, or perhaps used again to look at the stars at a millennium party. These are very much toys for the boys. Although women like them, it seems to be men who go for these objects.

This (right) is a refracting telescope made by Cook, a great maker. It has a high-quality ground glass lens at each end of the tube; the bigger lens is 20cm (8ins). It is the more commercial of the two telescopes shown because of the maker and also because of the technology; also, in many respects, it is more elegant with its long, solid brass tubing and extremely handsome.

I bought it after I got a call from a private person who said, in a broad Lancashire accent, 'I've got a telescope. Would you be interested?' He lived out on the East Lancashire Road in Manchester in a bungalow.

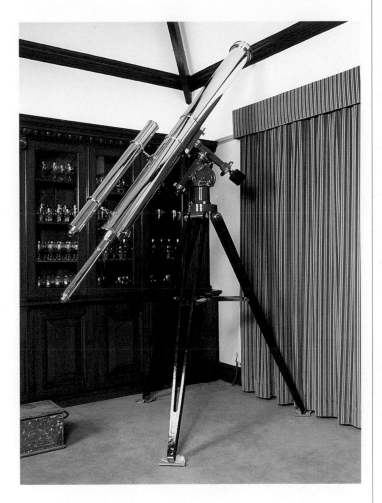

Sometimes such visits are a waste of time, but I went, and it just shows that life is full of surprises. When I arrived and said, 'Where's your telescope?' he led me into the back garden where he had built a small observatory, a large wooden shed-like

building with this huge telescope in it. It was incredible to find such an object in such a mundane environment, even though it was very tatty and had to be totally restored. My specialist took it apart, recleaned, polished and repaired all the brass, redid the stove enamelling and stripped all the mechanism. Eventually I sold it to a firm who are pipe fitters to use as an art object within their reception area.

This reflecting telescope (left) doesn't have the conventional lens: it's all done with a reflecting mirror, there are time clocks and complex settings – it's a technical piece of equipment. It came from a country house where in Victorian times the gentleman owner would have been a keen amateur astronomer. Even today this would stand up well against a contemporary telescope with modern lenses and plastics.

As it was in a fairly poor condition, I had the entire thing restored and stove-enamelled. You can see just from looking at the photograph what a handsome 'masculine' object it is, with strong dramatic lines and technical feel, that would fit well into a heavily panelled library or hall.

Globes

These are called library globes because that is what they were designed for. Often, they come in pairs: a terrestrial globe, which showed the world and frequently the shipping routes, and a celestial one which showed the heavens. The larger one (top right) by Johnston, is a late Victorian shipping globe dated 1900. The smaller one (bottom right) by Phillips, dated 1840, is also terrestrial and would have had a celestial partner. Today they make wonderful decorative items – at a price.

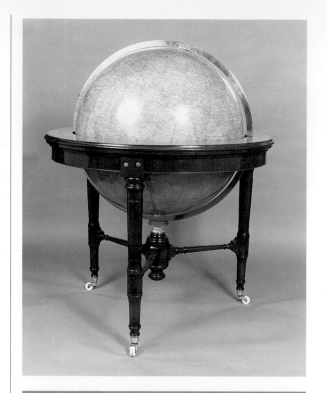

An Art Nouveau-style bronzed figure with glass globe

The lesson with this is: buy only if the glass is intact. The appearance of this piece is of a cast bronze figure, but it is in fact 'bronzed', that is, it has an applied bronze patination applied over spelter, a lighter, cheaper base metal. To my eyes it is a wonderful decorative object that can still be used for its original purpose, as a light. It is amazing that the glass shade or globe is intact, for so many of them just never made it. If it had been broken I would never have looked at it, since it is impossible to replace.

A set of Regency fairground scales

When we'd been in business for a few years at my first premises in Disley, Chris Haworth and I got something of a reputation as 'the boys' who bought great and unusual things. We were the new boys on the block, successful, making money, so there was a certain amount of jealousy. Lots of the local dealers wanted to take a rise out of us, perhaps to knock us down a peg or two or to make a good profit off us. One particular dealer called us up one day and, using a cunning ploy said, 'Come out to the house. I've got a clock I want to show you.' We arrived at his bungalow, went in, and there were some magnificent Regency brass scales, all original, filling the room. We thought we had come to see a clock but he knew he'd have us as soon as we walked in, and he did, hook, line and sinker. Instantly smitten, we said, 'How much do you want for them?'

He had bought them from a travelling fairground family who had owned them since the early 19th century, going from fair to fair around the country weighing people in the days before bathroom scales. Made by S. Walker and Co. of Sheffield, they were used until the 1950s and regularly checked by the weights and measures people, before eventually being wrapped in greased paper and put away, which kept them in perfect condition. I hadn't got a clue what they were worth, my gut instinct told me that they were rare, and that I'd never get another chance to buy something like this. I also knew that this guy was trying to take advantage of us. Laughing up his sleeve, he asked us for £2,800, and I think we haggled him down to £2,400. Later I heard that he had paid £800 for them. It was a lot of money for something that I wasn't sure what to do with, but they were so unique that I had to have them. We put them in our usual spot on the back of *Antiques Weekly* and immediately got a phone call from Paris from a Madame Brandycourt, a lady whom I later became friendly with and sold lots of goods to over the years. She had a fabulous shop just off the Champs Élysées. She said, 'The scales, they are wonderful – how much are they?' She told me that she wanted to exhibit them at the Paris Biennial, probably the most important fair in the world.

I took a deep breath and said, '£5,500'.

She said, 'Will £5,000 buy them?'

I said, 'Oui!'

It seemed an enormous profit, but I would not like to assess today with hindsight how much they are worth. I now know they are so rare that they should be in a museum. Since then I have seen parts of similar scales, but nothing as complete, with the flare lamps and all the right weights.

Blackamoors

Over the years blackamoors have become quite a speciality with me. Watching their prices spiral to dizzying heights has confirmed to me that *if your gut instinct tells you that something that you personally admire is going to rise rapidly in value, even if you can't afford it, buy it.* Soon you may be priced right out of the market and you may never get the chance again.

I advertised these blackamoors over a two- or three-year period on my usual back page of *Antiques Weekly* and got a very good response, which encouraged me to keep on buying blackamoors of every variety – as you see here, there are many kinds. Madam Brandycourt bought my very first pair. She sold them and bought them back, then I bought them back in turn from her and sold them to my Saudi business partner with whom I opened a large new shop in Manchester. He also bought two other pairs that I had, selling them on to his father, who at that time owned the Dorchester, where they are still. (This story also illustrates the fact that as antiques recycle it is hard for anyone to pull the wool over an old timer's eyes.)

This is Lorne on my stand at Olympia, showing off one of my largest and most spectacular Venetian Nubian blackamoors made of carved fruitwood. I was eventually able to track down the original invoice (bottom left), which raised the ante somewhat.

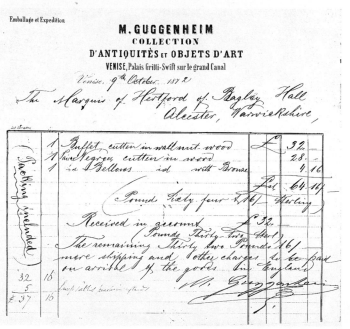

In the late 1970s I went to a Grosvenor House fair, the Ascot of the antiques world, and saw two huge pairs of Venetian blackamoor figures on loan from the Queen Mother. The general rule of thumb with pairs is that a pair is not twice the money but three times or more. These two pairs (not a quartet) were worth twice the value of one pair. A year or so later I acquired this (far left) single Nubian figure, originally one of a pair, in turban and Eastern attire, surmounted by an oval jardinière with wagon-handle sides and an ebonized turned hexagonal base, identical to those HM owned, so I wrote to her (as you do) asking her if she could supply me with any information on the provenance or the background of her figures. In due course, she replied (see letter right). Though they were catalogued in the 1950s, I now know that these probably date from the first part of the 19th century. My subsequent research unearthed the fact that the Marquis of Hertford, of Ragley Hall, Alcester in Warwickshire, also had a pair of virtually identical blackamoors. He passed me on to his secretary who looked in the archives and produced the original receipt of the pair that were supplied to the Marquis (opposite): 'One pair of Negroes cutten in wood – £28.00.' I sold mine to a client in the early 1980s and recently I bought it back, delighted to give him a profit, for the second time exhibiting it at Olympia. Art dealer Robin Hirlstone spotted it on my stand, approached me and said, 'I know where there are four of those.'

'Interesting, that,' I said, 'because I know where the four came from.' He was staying in a magnificent house in Barbados with his girlfriend, Joan Collins, when he spotted them. You don't think of the Queen Mother selling things, but obviously she does. She's quite a collector and sometimes has to make room for her latest acquisitions – in the same way as the rest of us.

CLARENCE HOUSE
S.W.1
2nd November, 1987

Dear Mr Dickinson

Queen Elizabeth The Queen Mother has asked me to write and thank you for your letter.

I am afraid that there is not a great deal I can tell you about the provenance of the Nubian figures.

They were acquired by The Queen Mother after a sale at Christies in February 1954. They were subsequently sold by Her Majesty in 1979, and I believe they have found a home in Barbados.

In case it would be of interest their description in the catalogue at Christies reads as follows: 'A set of four Venetian carved wood torcherers, carved as standing Nubian figures, wearing turbans and Eastern attire and supporting on their should turned pedestals, surmounted by oval jardinieres with dragon handles at the sides and lions' mask and ring handles to the centres, on ebonised turned hexagonal bases - about 7 ft. high - 18th century'.

Yours sincerely,

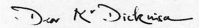

Comptroller to
Queen Elizabeth The Queen Mother

D. Dickinson, Esq.,

I sold this pair of exquisite female Venetian blackamoor torchères to a member of the Saudi royal family. Maybe it's the Armenian side of me that makes me love the dramatic look of the carved wood coated in gesso (plaster) with polychrome decoration – about 1840.

These, in the form of Egyptians, carved wood and gilded, today adorn the dining room of a Saudi international businessman, a former partner of mine. To buy a pair of these blackamoor *torchère* figures today you would expect to pay round about £25,000.

Another spectacular pair of polychrome decorated Venetian blackamoors, dating from the 19th century, which sold to an Armenian banker.

Black Forest knights

A pair of two-thirds life-size, carved walnut Black Forest knights (Austrian-German), these two figures are exceptionally commercial and probably only a king's ransom would buy them today. Wonderful decorative items, they were probably originally out of some fairy-tale Bavarian castle – something else I wish I had never sold.

Showman's traction engine

I have included this as a decorative object, because it is the kind of thing you don't often come across so would be snapped up by an industrial mogul for his corporate headquarters. But wouldn't it astonish some little boy to wake up on Christmas morning and find this in his stocking? A museum-quality, perfect, working quarter-size model, about 2m (6ft) long – a full-size one would have driven a fairground. It was the first expensive piece I ever bought for a princely £7,000. Another antiques dealer bought it from me at the first time I had a stand at Olympia for about £9,000. Today, I'd most likely need a maharaja's fortune to buy the engine back.

Exhibition-quality Furniture

This is the kind of furniture I especially admire. I have already discussed the Victorians and their astonishing furniture (see page 25). You could have snapped much of this up for paltry sums a few years back; today if they are not in the Victoria and Albert Museum they are out of reach of the average pocket. I realize that they are not little corner cupboards but if you're a beginner you can't do better than to study real quality, and here it shines out. I believe that there is a form of osmosis by which quality will soak in and you will acquire a sophisticated taste, just as I did. I also started small, and look where it got me.

Cabinet

Attributed to but not signed Jackson and Graham. Made of calamander (ebony family from the East Indies) with profusely inlaid exotic veneers and ivory. Mirrored door and shelf backs. Value in excess of £25,000.

Pair of cabinets

Attributed to Holland and Sons.
Made of golden amboyna wood
of a wonderful colour with
ebony stringing, Wedgwood
oval plaques and fine gilding.
Value £25,000 the pair.

Pair of vitrines

A vitrine is a display cabinet
that contains a great deal of
glass. We attributed these to
Jackson and Graham. Made of
ebony and ivory. Their former
value was in the region of
£35,000; it has risen since.

Cabinet

A neo-classical style stamped Wright and Mansfield; satinwood with the finest quality gilt bronze mounts and ovals with classical maidens painted on them. Value: £30,000.

Cabinet 1860

I attributed this to Wright and Mansfield although it was difficult to know since so many other exhibition-quality makers, such as Holland and Sons or Jackson and Graham are possible contenders. Satinwood inlaid with ivory – more magnificent in the flesh. Value: £45,000.

Cabinet, 1870

Stamped Lamb of Manchester. Walnut profusely inlaid with exotic woods, French Sèvres panels on the front and profusely decorated with gilt bronze. Magnificent. Value: £30,000.

Writing table, circa 1860

Stamped Holland and Sons. Satinwood and ebony with gilt and ormolu swags and decoration. Cloverleaf stretchers with gilt bronze central urn. Originally made for Chedgrave Manor, Norfolk. Value: £25,000.

Gillows

One of my favourite makers is Gillows. I think if any single furniture maker shines out from 1728 to the end of the Victorian period, it is the Gillows family of Lancaster, who were great innovators, making all types of furniture to the highest quality and workmanship.

19th-century Gillows writing table (bureau plat) circa 1860

Although there is a certain amount of Frenchness about this piece, with its gilt bronze mounts (note the rams' heads), it also has that Louis VX style about it in the cabriole legs. The English were producing writing tables to a similar style at the same time. Note also the profusely inlaid top: the main veneering is amboyna, lavishly inlaid with exotic veneers: boxwood, tulip wood and ebony. Value: £30,000 plus.

Gillows architect's pedestal desk with secretaire, circa 1790

This is more traditional Gillows. It has an architect's drawing-board top with double ratchet to adjust and a secretaire with writing surface inside. The top folds down and the secretaire pushes in and makes a traditional pedestal desk – overall a very clever design. Gillows were making Cuban mahogany furniture from the late 18th century right the way through into the 19th century. This is a fine late Georgian piece. Value: £20,000.

Bookcase, circa 1850–60

This is not stamped Gillows, but was attributed by us. It is a magnificently carved walnut piece with medieval-style heads and wonderful figuring. A slab of marble is placed on the top. Value: £30,000.

Inspirational Pieces

As I have mentioned before (see page 27) Victorian furniture makers often took their inspiration from both an earlier age and from the work of some of the greatest designers of all: Chippendale, Sheraton and Hepplewhite. At the time they were made, these Victorian pieces would have been 'reproductions' (much as high-quality reproductions are today), but, in the fullness of time, they have become antiques in their own right and in terms of quality, these are the *crème de la crème*.

19th-century Carlton-House-style desk

By repute the original of this desk was made for the Prince Regent at his home, Carlton House in London, which is why this style is called Carlton House. I have seen many late 19th-century Carlton House-style desks that were much more delicate; this one was very much a man's desk, as is emphasized by the rich colour and quality of the glowing Cuban mahogany veneers, in the manner of the original, which would have been dated round about 1790. This example (dated late 19th century) has all the hallmarks of quality: the veneer figuring, a wonderful matching veneer 'flame,' cast brass handles, Brahma locks. The original leather was there (always try to get the original leather whenever possible and restore it even if it costs – see page 123).

I exhibited this piece at Olympia and sold it to an enthusiastic farmer from Shropshire, who fell in love with it at first sight. About an hour later a rather swarthy gentleman approached the stand with a large retinue, and asked me about the desk and how much it was.

I told him the price and added that it was sold.

He then repeated himself, saying again, 'How much is it?'

I said, 'Well, sir, as I

mentioned to you, it is sold.'

His response was to say, 'I didn't ask you that – how much is it?'

I took a deep breath to explain it all again patiently, and one of the retinue stepped forward and handed me a card. I won't say which Middle East royal family the card identified him as from. The equerry seemed aghast that a refusal was being made.

Obviously thinking I was being deliberately obtuse, the prince changed his question, asking, 'How much will you take for it?'

Again I explained, 'I'm sorry, but two hours ago this was sold to a farmer in Shropshire.'

He seemed quite taken aback; nobody refuses one of these mega-rich princes from the Gulf states where money is no object. His entire demeanour was, 'How much has it got to be? I want it!' He just couldn't grasp that I wasn't trying to push the price up, that the piece was sold, end of story. There was a confused look in his eyes as the penny dropped. The entourage were looking nervous: here was a man refusing HRH.

Eventually a smile came to his face when I suggested, 'If Your Royal Highness is really

interested, I could ask the farmer to give you a ring, but I must warn you they're a canny lot down in Shropshire and he probably won't want to sell it to you anyway.'

Money isn't everything. The canny farmer drove a hard bargain with me and took this highly desirable desk home, and the prince from the Gulf states didn't get it, and wasn't likely to get it either.

Display cabinet, circa 1890

Mahogany Chinese Chippendale-style revival with the most exquisite ornate carving and fretwork. This is a piece piece that gives a wonderfully delicate impression.

Console table

Mahogany, Sheraton-style
revival with an ornate marble
top. Note the lavish use of
carved wooden swags around
the apron and the reeded
tapered rectangular legs.

Figures

The piece that Michael Jackson didn't get

This is a charming marble sculpture of two lovers, a shepherd and shepherdess, by Vichi, an exceptionally talented Italian artist. I managed to buy it in a country house sale, with half the London trade there trying to buy it at the same time. Some London dealers who did quite a lot of business with the pop star Michael Jackson had previously sold him a similar Vichi piece, *Romeo and Juliet in Florentine Costume*. Knowing that I had bought *The Lovers* at a sale, they asked if I would send it down to them on sale or return, as Michael was due in London. He always came to see them and they were sure he would buy this the moment he set eyes on it. I said I would send it to them, but only if they bought it from me. 'I took the risk of acquiring it in the first place,' I pointed out. 'You want me to send it to you at my expense. If he buys it you'll slap a huge profit on it which I won't see –

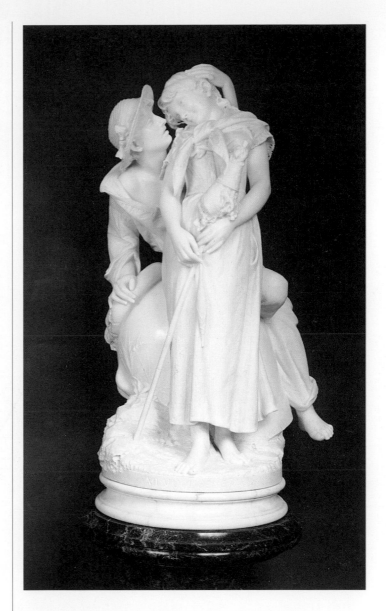

and if he doesn't buy it, I have to pay to ship it home. I took a chance – so must you.' The dealers were adamant – they still wanted it on sale or return – so unfortunately Michael didn't get the chance to buy it. Instead, I sold it to a director of a Nile cruise company and it went to Egypt.

Friedrich Goldscheider

From Vienna in the late 19th century, Goldscheider pieces are a particular favourite and speciality of mine, not only because of the quality of Goldscheider's work, but also because of the delightful and witty subjects he often chose. The rising prices of his work reflects these attributes. Today, you are lucky if you can find a signed Goldscheider piece almost at any price. I have had several and wish I could have kept them all. Superficially like bronzes, they are bronzed and painted terracotta. Many of them are life-size or nearly so.

A Negro dandy, circa 1890

Perhaps my favourite Goldscheider piece, made in terracotta, is this Negro with a metal monocle in his eyes, seated on a real bamboo chair. About 35cm (14ins) high, this is both desirable and very fashionable because it is so decorative. I love the angle of his straw hat and his feet in the stylish shoes – you can almost hear them tapping out a tune. Note his large gold cuff links and watch fob – he's quite a dandy. One of these today in perfect condition unrestored is likely to sell for not less than £2,500–£3,000.

Gone Fishin' circa 1890

Don't you just love the cheek and humour of this life-size bronzed terracotta boy? With a real wood fishing pole and chair, bare feet, ragged clothes, his hat turned sideways (long before it was trendy to push your baseball cap around) and the fag end stuck in his widely smiling mouth, he's a regular Huckleberry Finn. A real find – you wouldn't buy one of these today under £10,000.

Arab boy with flute, circa 1890

Large – about 1.4m (4ft 6ins) – this Goldscheider piece is a tranquil polychrome terracotta figure with a bronzed finish. This Arab boy is dressed in a loose garment with a little red cap, completely lost in his music. This is another very expensive piece.

Sitting dog, circa 1890

This life-size dog – 1.25m (4ft) high – has such an alert and lively expression that you'd swear he was alive. His body hair, his bright eyes and even the pads of his feet are wonderfully executed, and I love the way his tail curls up. His pose, lolling slightly sideways on his haunches, makes him friendly rather than threatening; his expression seems to say, 'Don't forget I want to go for a walk!'

A Last Word

If you've reached this final page and have learned a few useful tips along the way, we will have both achieved a lot. By now, I hope, you will have a basic steering knowledge of buying antiques. I haven't finished with the tips though. Here's a last piece of advice. *Don't get too cocky; remember, you're still going to make mistakes*, exactly as I did (and sometimes still do). But making them will be the best part of your training. The more mistakes you make, the more they start to hit you in your pocket and the more sleepless nights you have, the more you are learning. Ultimately, of course, you will learn to restrict those mistakes; to make fewer and fewer.

And here's a final warning. If you happen to be in the saleroom clutching a copy of this book, bidding fast and furiously, and you hear someone calling across the room, 'Go on, buzz off!' it will probably be me. I may have turned you into something of an expert but I can guarantee that I have a few other tricks up my sleeve that you won't know about.

Jargon

Terminology, slang and expressions used within the antiques trade and by David Dickinson

What is jargon?

Whether you race horses, grow orchids or work in the rag trade, all walks of life have their own special terminology, developed over many years. To those in the know, their meaning is instantly clear and is often a kind of shorthand for description, value, condition and even of history that lies beneath the surface. The antiques trade is no different. Dealers and experts use flowery terminology and many subtle expressions which might confuse the uninitiated – and in fact, they are often intended to confuse or mislead. In catalogues your eye might just pass over such innocent-sounding terms as 'associated parts' – so I always advise people to really read every word in a catalogue that describes a piece they are interested in – and to question those throwaway phrases: they are not as innocent as they seem.

I also have a few terms of my own that I frequently use. Although some dealers might like to keep the mysteries of jargon within the trade, like some kind of Freemasons' secret language, really, there is no mystery – it's just our normal, everyday conversation. The following is a brief list of such expressions, with their meanings, that might make the beginner feel a little more involved when learning this fascinating business.

Associated parts

With associated parts is just a flowery way of saying the thing isn't right, that's it has bits from somewhere else added to it. Sometimes the expression is 'with added parts'; 'with alterations'; 'some renewals' or 'elements of a later date'. All are just other ways of saying something is an allsorts or a marriage, though there are some subtle nuances – for example, the 'associated parts' might equally be a new chair leg to replace one that was broken or a replacement weight on a long case clock or another set of drawer handles to a bureau. It's not going to sound very nice saying, '18th farmhouse table but played about with and parts replaced.' whereas 'A fine 18th farmhouse table with elements of a later date,' sounds more than acceptable. Without further information, when you see any of these phrases in a catalogue you should keep running and don't stop.

'Basically'

Saying something is 'basically 18th century' is another way of saying that it's not right. When you look in a catalogue at an auction and something is listed as being, 'basically an 18th century bureau' you should ask yourself, 'well what's the rest of it made of then?' It's just flannel for some pretty heavy restoration.

Bought in

The majority of pieces in the saleroom have a *reserve price* (see page 91) that has been negotiated and agreed or advised by the auctioneer beforehand. If they do not reach that reserve price the auctioneer withdraws it from offer.

Circa

Approximately or around about a certain date. 'Circa 1840' could mean ten or even fifteen years in either direction. Because a catalogue tells you that something is 'circa 1900' it doesn't necessarily mean it is always right. In the majority of cases it will be – but in my experience you have to use your own judgement in such circumstances.

A commercial lot

Something that is is readily saleable, even amongst the trade. It is something with a lot of commercial appeal that is usually attributable to the maker, as shown by a signature or a pasted label or some kind of a receipt.

Cut down

Here, there has been a

conversion from a large piece to a smaller piece. Sometimes (apart from filling a certain sized space) cutting down can make a large, clumsy piece superficially much more attractive and desirable, at least, to look at in proportion to modern smaller rooms. For example, tables have often been cut down to coffee table height and sold as original antiques. But coffee tables are a fairly recent invention; previously there might have been opium tables, usually of brass or marble – so don't be fooled. I believe it is the kiss of death to cut a piece down. I would always advise you to *stay away* from something that has been hacked about because, apart from the fact that it is not what it was originally made as (and one only has to look at it to realise that it stands wrong) the resale value will be low.

Decoration refreshed

It's a good phrase for dealers or in an auction catalogue because it sounds so harmless. It could mean some light touching here and there to paintwork or to gilding – or it could mean the whole nine yards has been heavily revamped and not a scrap of the original surface still remains.

Desirable

This is something which every one wants at that particular moment for whatever reason. It might be voguish or fashionable, or it will have a combination of good points such as nice design, good materials, it sits right, it is small and will fit into most modern homes or it is very useful, such as a table lamp or a mirror. We often say such items are 'commercial and highly desirable' when they will sell easily and hence will fetch a higher price.

Distressed

This can mean something that has really been knocked about. It can be restored but often this isn't worth the trouble. Or, in decorator's jargon, it can mean a modern piece that has been banged about and the corners rubbed to fake an antique appearance.

Estimate

This is a guideline price in a sale room catalogue which is not necessarily the price it will finish at. Usually an estimate has been agreed by the vendor who has been guided by the auctioneer, based on current market trends and his experience of what similar goods have fetched. Sometimes goods do not fetch their estimate and are *bought in* (see page 182) – or they might go wildly above it.

Fresh goods

Goods that are new to the market-place or that have not been seen in the trade. A piece that has probably spent its long life in a private home with one family and has never been up for sale before. This makes it more desirable to dealers – we all want to be the first to lay our hands on it and add it to our stock. Dealers often recognise pieces that circulate; they have a history and a provenance that can be traced and proved, very much like the blood-line of a race horse. While this adds value to good pieces, for poorer-quality items, there is a stigma to having been kicked around from dealer to saleroom and back again.

Honest

Similar to fresh goods; though fresh goods could have been altered, restored or repaired at some stage. We often say: '*it's an honest piece*' to describe something which is untouched, unrestored and fresh to the market. What you see is what you get – the piece is, solid, straightforward, well-made, in its original condition with no restoration or faking.

Liquorice allsorts

This means a piece is a mixture often patched up from two or more other items to make something else, such as doors from here and feet from there and a top from somewhere else. Such pieces are rarely fakes because they don't usually set out to deliberately mislead; rather, they are something that is supposed to look generally 'old' (as in Tudor, or Regency) and not anything specific. But often they end up looking like a dog's dinner. We often say of some appalling mish-mash, 'that's a real allsorts' or 'it's a real old mixture' or 'it's a marriage'.

Makeover job

This means that something has been over-refurbished or restored. Chairs might have been recovered or re-upholstered; glass and beading might have been replaced on a display cabinet or a bookcase; new handles and new gilding might have been added to a commode and so forth.

A marriage

This is one kind of marriage that you should avoid like the plague. It's when separate parts have been put together that never started life together. Anyone with half an eye can clearly see that such pieces are made from two or more different objects. For example, perhaps a large Welsh dresser might have been split up in the past because it was too large. A dealer comes along and he has the top from one dresser and the bottom of another. On their own these two parts are worth little – so he decides to put them together in the hopes of persuading a customer into

parting company with a substantial sum. Such a piece is not really a fake as such because its intrinsic parts are original; they are not made up and aged to look like an antique – but you would not buy a car that has been welded together from half a Vauxhall and half a Ford. As I often say, such marriages are not made in heaven and should be left well alone.

A paint job

This could include a piece of furniture that has been heavily repaired and well stained or varnished to hide the fact; or it has been re-lacquered, which often conceals the fact that two pieces that don't belong together have been patched together. You could be looking at a superficial paint job on top of an 1800s cupboard – or a great deal of camouflage on something that is 1960s. You would have to inspect it pretty thoroughly to tell. This term could also include ceramics that have been repaired, repainted and then refired. (See, for example, page 109 – how to tell if bisque has been repaired.)

Patination

This is the many decades and centuries of handling and wear and polish that gives an antique piece its irreplaceable surface colour and finish. Sometimes called a skin, as in, '*it's got a good skin on it*' patination

applies to furniture as well as to silver. In the case of silver, the removal of minescule amounts of silver during the cleaning process lends the piece myriads of scratches over the centuries which seems to lend it a unique, almost silky glow which cannot be faked.

Period

Relating to the exact historical period in which something was made. For example, Chippendale chairs were designed in the 18th century, so that is their period; but many other contemporaneous furniture makers copied pieces from Chippendale's directory, and those pieces, while not Chippendale, are known as of that period.

In period

A piece of furniture or decorative goods that are of the period in which it they were made. For example Carolinian chairs indicate chairs of a certain style and wood associated with the reign of Charles and made in the 17th century. Any similar pieces made afterwards would be Carolinian *style*; and equally, Chippendale style or Hepplewhite style and so on. They are still valid as antiques in their own right, perhaps not worth as much as the originals, but still worth collecting. For instance, if you buy a piece of Regency furniture, it was made during the Regency period which would be about 1800–1830. Anything similar made outside those days is 'Regency style'.

Out of period

This indicates antique pieces that are of the same style, but not of the same period as the originals. You often see 'Chippendale' chairs that were not made by Thomas Chippendale, nor at the period in which he lived. These pieces are to his design but made at another time, perhaps 100 years later. Technically speaking, they are reproductions – but antique reproductions (that is, pieces more than 100 years old) – and have an intrinsic value of their own. We don't call them reproduction, because that suggests something very modern. Their correct description would be something like: '19th-century chairs in a Chippendale style.'

Provenance

The proven history and background to a piece that adds to its value. The provenance can include an original receipt; inclusion in a furniture maker's catalogue; an old sales or exhibition catalogue; the inventory of a great house; or a signature somewhere on it.

Recycled goods

If these were not antiques, many of them would be called 'second-hand'. They are goods that keeps on circulating through the antiques trade, often from dealers. By and large you don't want them – because nobody else does.

Reserve price

This is the lowest price that the vendor will accept in an auction. If the bidding does not reach this amount, then the auctioneer cannot sell the piece and is obliged to turn down the highest bid.

Restoration to surface

This could mean anything. Perhaps the odd bit of veneer has been replaced – or an old carcase has been completely redone. Ask an expert exactly how much of the original piece remains.

Revival

This is very similar to a piece being *of the style of,* or *out of period.* However, it suggests more a resurgence of a certain fashion which suddenly becomes all the rage. The pieces created are usually not exact copies of the originals – there are always subtle differences by which they can be dated and which reflect new sensibilities and styles. For example, the Regency look was influenced by Greek and Roman architecture and patterns. Many of the designs that were used in the

18th century were revived in the 19th century and had subtle Victorian nuances; while the Pre-Raphaelites at the end of the Victorian period revived a kind of romantic Italian Gothic look.

There have been several revivals over the centuries. Where antiques are concerned, the date of the revival affects the value, depending on whether it is 50 or 100 or 200 years later. The earlier, the better it is considered to be. A 1930 revival of a Queen Anne bureau might be worth £1500; nowhere near as valuable as an 1820s Regency revival – while the real thing from 1702 might be worth upwards of £80,000.

Signed

Paintings aren't the only valuable goods that are signed. Often furniture-makers engraved their names on a piece, or glued a label to the back or inside. Ceramics, silver and metalwork have stamped or painted marks and even glass can have a signature engraved somewhere. Often you will hear an expert say something has a signature (even when unsigned) when what they mean is that it can be identifiable as a particular artist or maker's work because of an instantly recognisable style or technique.

A sleeper

A piece which is underrated and is more desirable than people think it is. It is something the value and desirability of which has not been recognised by the vendor or the valuer. So it has been catalogued and put into the saleroom as something perhaps quite ordinary with a modest or low estimate. Then low and behold, when people in the trade come along one or more instantly recognises its true value. They hope to keep it just to themselves, but dealers seem to have an almost telepathic knowledge of what is interesting and they are drawn like magnets from far and wide. The next thing is, there is quite a buzz going on and when the piece comes up, there can be fierce competition for it (see the Regency writing desk story on page 174).

Stands well

When a piece of furniture 'stands well' it looks balanced. The whole design to your eye is balanced and in harmony. This comes from experience; but even an amateur can tell if something doesn't look quite right, even if they don't know precisely why.

Studio of

If we say a piece is **by** someone (as in '*by Rubens*') that means that there is no doubt that it was created by him. If *attributed to* it means it was more than likely by him, but there is no signature so there might be some doubt.

Studio or *Circle of* means that the work was produced by pupils or apprentices who were working under the master's umbrella, in his studio. Some artists were apparently so prolific that we now know that they could not possibly have had the time to paint all that was attributed to them. They would have outlined a painting, or made the model for a statue – and some talented lad would have done three-quarters of the balance, with the master stepping in for the final touches and to put his stamp on it. Who did what on many valuable pieces has become a bone of contention with the experts.

In the style of

This relates to furniture and works of art, such as paintings or sculptures, that are similar to or influenced by the work of a great artist but not done in his studio, nor by his pupils, but by another artist altogether, perhaps in another period.

THE FOLLOWING ARE A FEW OF MY OWN PERSONAL FAVOURITE EXPRESSIONS.

That's a cracking lot

This is a piece of my own particular jargon. Sometimes I say, '*what a great piece of kit*', reflecting my enthusiasm for something in very good condition that is a perfect example of its type and period.

As rare as hen's teeth

Something rare and unusual, hardly ever seen in the trade (see page 109 for an example)

Rolls Royce

We say something is a Rolls Royce when we mean it is quality – quite simply the best example you could find.

A great looker

A very good-looking piece of furniture or decorative item that has all the attributes of style and quality.

It could be anything

When you look at piece and haven't a clue what you are looking at – the word liquorice allsorts springs to mind.

Further Reading

There is a book for every subject under the sun and, excepting extremely quirky subjects, usually many. Often, there will be at least one inexpensive introductory book and one definitive tome. Once you are certain that you have found an abiding interest in a particular area of antiques or collectables, it is worth investing in the tome. You can search second-hand bookshops as an alternative to buying it new – while doing so, you may well find other excellent books on your subject, which are now unfortunately out of print. Look in the bibliography section of the tome for further reading.

Bookshops and libraries are excellent places to browse through a wide range of books on antiques but choose the right ones. Go for the main library rather than the branch; go for the biggest bookshop you can get to or specialist art bookshops – in particular, try those at the leading decorative arts museums (e.g. The Victoria & Albert Museum, London; the Fitzwilliam, Cambridge; the Ashmolean, Oxford).

There may well be a collectors' club in your subject: ask around. A good general one is the Antique Collectors' Club (5 Church Street, Woodbridge, Suffolk IP12 1DS) which publishes a range of authoritative books. NADFAS – the National Association of Decorative and Fine Arts Societies – may well have a branch in your area, providing monthly talks by experts on a range of subjects (HQ is 8 Guildford Street, London WC1; tel 0181 430 0730). Some collectors' clubs are able to provide publications at a reasonable discount.

If you have access to it, the Internet may provide a good source of information on your subject. You would certainly be able to contact on-line bookshops such as the American pair of Amazon (http://www.amazon.com) or Barnes and Noble (http://www.barnesandnoble.com) which often have cut-price offers or British ones such as Blackwells (http://www.blackwells.co.uk) or Waterstones (http://www.waterstones.co.uk), which also offers a book search for out-of-print stock. Of course, they do not allow you to simply take a book off the shelf and get an idea of its contents.

Then you could explore museums with your subject in mind. The address for a directory of museums sorted by country is http://www.icom.org/vimp/world.html.

Especially in America, Web-swapping and trading of collectables is extremely lively, but beware: a lot of people have been burned this way. It's safer to enjoy observing what goes on but to stick to time-honoured ways of buying and selling.

POTTERY & PORCELAIN

STARTING OUT

The Concise Guide to British Pottery & Porcelain, Geoffrey Godden, 1990

The Handbook of British Pottery & Porcelain Marks, Geoffrey Godden, 1975

Collecting Pottery & Porcelain by Janet Gleeson et al, 1997

Antique Porcelain, John Sandon, 1997

SERIOUS STUFF

Encyclopaedia of British Pottery & Porcelain, Geoffrey Godden, 1968

Encyclopaedia of British Pottery & Porcelain Marks, Geoffrey Godden, 1964

David Battie's Guide to Understanding 19th and 20th Century British Porcelain, 1994

The Dictionary of Blue and White Printed Pottery 1780–1880, AW Coysh and R K Henrywood, 1982

SPECIALIST STUFF

The subject of ceramics illustrates very well how some interests sub-divide into what seems, from a distance, a very small subject area. Get closer and you discover that the 'small' subject area, Art Deco say, can be divided into even smaller zones of interest – a particular designer or make or country. This is not a comprehensive list and some of these titles are just overviews, but is intended to show how well almost every taste is catered for by publishers. The same principle applies to just about every collecting area, but is, because of sheer quantity made and its conveniently collectable size, perhaps particularly relevant to ceramics.

Christie's Collectables: Art Deco China, Jane Hay, 1996

Christie's Collectables: Teapots, Paul Tippet, 1996

Coalport 1795–1926, Michael Messenger, 1995

Coalport Figurines, Gaye Blake-Roberts, 1997

Collecting Carlton Ware, David Serpell, 1998

Collecting Doulton Animals, Jocelyn Lukins, 1990

English Earthenware Figures 1740–1840, Pat Halfpenny, 1991

The Dictionary of Minton, Paul Atterbury and Maureen Batkin, 1990

Moorcroft, Paul Atterbury, 1990

Wedgwood: A Collector's Guide, Peter Williams, 1992

Chinese Ceramics, He Li, 1996

Egg Cups: an illustrated history and price guide, Brenda Blake, 1995

SILVER & METALWORK

STARTING OUT

English Silver Hallmarks, Dealer Guide, Judith Banister, 1995

Sotheby's Concise Encyclopaedia of Silver, Charles Truman et al, 1996

Starting to Collect Silver, John Luddington, 1984

Antique Silver Identifier, Lydia Darbyshire, 1994

SERIOUS STUFF

Jackson's Silver & Gold Marks of England, Scotland and Ireland, Ian Pickford, 1989

The National Trust Book of English Domestic Silver, Timothy Schroder, 1988

Forks, Knives and Spoons, Peri Wolfman and Charles Gold, 1994

Domestic Metalwork 1640–1820, Rupert Gentle and Rachel Feild, 1994

Phaidon Guide to Pewter, Vanessa Brett, 1981*

FURNITURE

STARTING OUT

Starting to Collect Antique Furniture, John Andrews, 1997

Furniture, A Concise History, Edward Lucie-Smith, 1979*

Furniture, Judith and Martin Miller, 1991

Miller's Pine and Country Furniture Buyer's Guide, Judith and Martin Miller, 1995

SERIOUS STUFF

British Antique Furniture Price Guide and Reasons for Values, John Andrews, 1989

Pictorial Dictionary of British 19th Century Furniture Design, Antique Collectors' Club, 1977

Western Furniture 1350 to the Present Day, edited Christopher Wilk, 1996

Hepplewhite, Sheraton & Regency Furniture, F. Lewis Hinckley, 1990

Biedermeier Furniture with Values, Rudolf Pressler/Robin Straub, 1996

Identifying American Furniture, Milo M. Naeve, 1998

GLASS

English Glassware to 1900, Charles Truman, 1984*

Glass Through the Ages, E. Barrington Haynes, 1948*

Glass, Mark West, 1994

Sotheby's Concise Encyclopaedia of Glass, Coral Mula and Robert J Charleston, 1994

CARPETS

STARTING OUT

Rugs & Carpets of the World, Ian Bennet, 1977*

Oriental Carpet Identifier, Ian Bennet, 1985

SERIOUS STUFF

Oriental Rugs: series from the Antique Collector's Club:

Volume 1 Caucasian

Volume 2 Persian

Volume 3 Afghanistan

Volume 4 Turkish

Volume 5 Turkoman

TOYS

STARTING OUT

Collins Gem *Dolls*; Collins Gem *Teddy Bears*, 1997

200 Years of Dolls: Identification and Price Guide, Dawn Herlocher, 1996

SPECIALIST

100 Tin Toys, Teruhisa Kitahara and Yukio Shimuzu, 1996

British Model Trains, John Ramsay, 1997

Christie's World of Automotive Toys, Mike and Sue Richardson, 1998

The Dinky Toy Price Guide, Frank Thompson, 1995

Toy Soldiers, Andrew Rose, 1997

Teddy Bears Identifier, Margaret and Gerry Grey, 1996

The Ultimate Doll Book, Caroline Goodfellow, 1993

GENERAL

The Little-Brown Illustrated Encyclopaedia of Antiques, Lars Tharp and Paul Atterbury, 1994

Miller's Antiques Encyclopaedia, ed. Judith Miller, 1998

The Penguin Dictionary of Decorative Arts, John Fleming and Hugh Honour, 1989

Phaidon Encyclopaedia of Decorative Arts 1890–1940, ed. Philippe Garnier, 1978

'Reader's Digest' Treasures in Your Home, 1997

The Which Guide to Buying Antiques

Antiques Clinic: a collector's guide to diagnosing damage, the possibilities of restoration and care for the future, James Fielden, Richard Garnier, Paul Davidson and Bruce Luckhurst, 1999

Illustrated History of Antiques, ed. Huon Mallalieu, 1993

The Country Life Pocket Book of Collector's Terms, Therle Hughes, 1979*

The Antiques Market Browser's Marks Guide, 1977

The Which Guide to Buying Collectables, Duncan Chilcott, 1991

300 Years of Kitchen Collectables, Linda Campbell Franklin, 1998

Antiques from the Garden, Alistair Morris, 1996

Yesterday's Children, the Antiques and History of Childcare, Sally Kevill-Davies, 1991

British Coins Market Values annuals

The entire Shire Album Series, on subjects as diverse as early plastics, gramophones or snuff boxes: small, thorough and cheap

MEMORABILIA

From the Beatles to Beanie Babies; from tin trays to tins; from cigarette cards to cigar wrappers to comics: there will be a book or a web site, however amateur. Just keep looking. If you really can't find one, there's a gap in the market: perhaps you should write it!

*This denotes books that are out-of-print but still worth including as they are still very good books if you can get them.

Index